Sales Strategy for Business Growth

Julian Clay and Martin Clay

THOROGOOD

Published by Thorogood Publishing
10-12 Rivington Street
London EC2A 3DU
Telephone: 020 7749 4748
Fax: 020 7729 6110
Email: info@thorogoodpublishing.co.uk
Web: www.thorogoodpublishing.co.uk

© Julian Clay and Martin Clay 2013

All rights reserved. No part of this publication may be reproduced, stored in a retrieval system or transmitted in any form or by any means, electronic, photocopying, recording or otherwise, without the prior permission of the publisher.

Every effort has been made to trace and acknowledge the owners of various pieces of material in this publication. If further proof of ownership should be made available then attribution will be given or, if requested, the said material removed in any subsequent editions.

The right of Julian Clay and Martin Clay to be identified as the authors of this work has been asserted in accordance with the Copyright, Designs and Patents Act 1988.

This book is sold subject to the condition that it shall not, by way of trade or otherwise, be lent, re-sold, hired out or otherwise circulated without the publisher's prior consent in any form of binding or cover other than in which it is published and without a similar condition including this condition being imposed upon the subsequent purchaser.

A CIP catalogue record for this book is available from the British Library.

ISBN 1854187961 · 9781854187963

Book designed and typeset in the UK by Driftdesign

Printed and bound in Great Britain by Marston Book Services Limited, Didcot

Special discounts for bulk quantities of Thorogood books are available to corporations, institutions, associations and other organisations. For more information contact Thorogood by telephone on: 020 7749 4748, by fax on: 020 7729 6110, or email us: info@thorogoodpublishing.co.uk

About the Authors

Julian Clay

Julian has an honours degree in Psychology and Business Studies and was a top sales performer and senior manager in Kodak's Office Imaging division. Since leaving in 1998 he has worked with a large number of different types and size of companies. He is now part of a well established business management practice, EMC Management Consultants.

His key strengths involve working with companies in order for them to achieve growth. This has included helping them to develop a sales strategy, sales processes, coaching people and working as an interim sales director. He has also written and delivered many successful sales training programmes.

His expertise lies in understanding the core business challenges faced by companies, as well as having the ability to assess and build on a sales team's skills. He has developed a sales forecasting software programme to help companies manage and win more business opportunities.

Julian is also the co-author of *The Sales Manager's Desktop Guide* and author of *Successful Selling Solutions* (both published by Thorogood).

Martin Clay

Martin has an MBA and has worked in a sales environment for over 20 years. This has included key roles at world-class organisations such as Xerox and Panasonic.

He was also part of the sales team at Capital Software when it was recognised by *The Independent on Sunday* awards. This award confirmed Capital Software as one of the United Kingdom's *50 Fastest Growing Companies*.

As sales manager of this software recruitment company, Martin was involved in the strategic planning during their expansion across Europe. He was described as 'an inspirational and motivating sales leader who has an exceptional ability to engage customers and colleagues.'

In addition to a successful sales career, Martin writes and delivers business 'start-up' training courses. He also teaches Business Studies and Economics and lectures with the Open University Business School.

Thanks

I would like to thank my wife, Zoe, for her unwavering support. I dedicate this book to her and my children: Edward, Dylan and Lily.

*****

We would both like to thank EMC Management Consultants Ltd for its co-operation and support in helping to publish this book.

Foreword

For the best part of a quarter of a century, EMC has been helping small and medium-sized businesses in the South East of England to survive through the bad times and thrive in the good... and occasionally vice-versa! Along the way we have created dozens of millionaires by helping business owners to build successful companies that we have sold for them when the time was right.

Most of our work is a hands-on, day-to-day involvement either as interim managers or trusted advisers across all the main business disciplines – finance, sales, marketing, IT and so on. But, inevitably, that can have its limitations. Our 'mobile boardroom' of experienced professionals can only deal with a certain number of client companies at any one time. So, we were delighted when Julian Clay joined our team and invited us to be part of this publishing venture. It enables Julian and his brother Martin, to share their knowledge and expertise in the vital area of sales strategy and management with a much wider audience.

Julian already has two highly successful books on sales management and selling skills under his belt and we're certain that this book will be equally well received. We're also working with him on another book on how to successfully manage business change issues.

The sales operation is not always the main focus for business owners, yet it is arguably the most important part of any company. This book details the actions owner-directors should take to ensure that their sales strategy looks to maximise growth and develop employees' potential.

Follow the book's advice and we're confident you will see a marked improvement in your company's sales performance.

Nik Askaroff
Chief Executive
EMC Management Consultants Ltd
www.emcltd.co.uk

Contents

About the Authors	3
Foreword	5
Introduction	10
Glossary of sales terms	13

Chapter 1
Responding to changes in the market	16
Identifying economic and market influences	17
Adapting a company's sales culture	28
Chapter summary	39

Chapter 2
Creating a sales and marketing strategy	42
Defining your marketing objectives	43
Analysing your sales performance	50
Effective branding	56
Chapter summary	73

Chapter 3
Implementing your strategy (with a sales operations plan)	76
Evaluating performance	77
Short, medium and long-term planning	86
Preparing for change	93
Chapter summary	99

Chapter 4
Getting the best out of a sales CRM system — 102
Managing sales information effectively — 103
Combining data and knowledge to create value — 109
Chapter summary — 118

Chapter 5
How to improve your decision-making — 120
Understanding behaviour — 121
How your management style can improve sales performance — 132
Chapter summary — 138

Chapter 6
A strategy to manage different types of people — 142
Management styles and forms of control — 143
Overcoming different sales challenges — 150
Knowing the personality types you manage — 154
Chapter summary — 164

Chapter 7
Teamwork and communication — 168
Working as part of a team — 169
Being assertive — 178
Communication skills — 183
Chapter summary — 189

Chapter 8
Working more productively — 192
Work/life balance — 193
Roles and responsibilities — 202
Chapter summary — 206

Bibliography — 208

Introduction

Introduction

This book is primarily designed to help business owners formulate and implement a successful sales strategy. The world is changing extremely quickly, with ever more competition entering different markets and making use of advancing technology.

With so much choice, adding real value and building good business relationships can be a real differentiator. This is why consumers often put demands on companies to supply products and services faster, better and at a lower cost. Responding to these changing expectations and making the most of the opportunities presented to a company will determine how successful it will be.

Understanding how a sales team operates within a changing environment and having a proactive approach will have a big impact on a company's future success. The ideas in this book will appeal to:

Business owners who may not have had any formal sales or management training and others who may want to review their existing sales strategy or improve its implementation.

Directors who want to learn more about how members of a sales team work so they can understand the barriers and opportunities which impact on the strategic direction of the company.

Sales managers who currently manage a sales team and who want to improve their understanding of the economic, sales, marketing, planning and behavioural side to management in order to increase sales effectiveness.

The book takes into consideration some of the daily themes which any business owner has to deal with. These include:

- Managing time constraints and a change of priorities.
- Dealing with interruptions.
- Getting involved with the demands of operational issues which deflect attention away from strategic sales planning.
- Reacting to short-term events without understanding the impact on long-term decision-making.
- Making the most of limited resources in order to compete with larger companies.
- Delegating tasks to people but not having checks in place to ensure they are always carried out correctly.

An important challenge for business owners is that many will not have come from a sales background. This can mean that they may not always be sure how to adapt to managing – or being responsible for – a sales team in order to meet the company's sales targets.

The key benefit of reading this book will be better sales performance achieved through improved decision-making. Its unique selling point is that every chapter is supported by evidence from eminent people including economists, psychologists and marketing experts.

The chapter topics are drawn from original sources, often not covered in a business or sales performance book. This is combined with tables and templates, which you can recreate and use in your everyday role, and ideas that will allow you to enhance your skills. This will give you a unique insight into how you can develop your sales operation and other parts of your company in order to successfully achieve sales growth.

The book starts by looking at the external business environment and how you can respond to it. This is an area which is often difficult to control (e.g. the effect of the economy or how to stay ahead of your competitors). It then moves on to how business owners can improve their internal sales environment and processes (e.g. management controls and communication styles).

Many of the chapters give advice which can be related to other departments which interact with the sales operation. The book will help business owners increase their chances of succeeding in their working environment. It will enable companies to increase their sales revenue and profitability by looking for practical solutions to key sales and marketing issues.

Note: To maintain uniformity, the term 'business owner' will be referred to throughout the book. However, many of the topics being discussed, as highlighted earlier, could be equally relevant to directors or sales managers.

Glossary of sales terms

Sales term	Meaning
SME	Small and Medium-sized Enterprise. **Small** – up to 50 employees. **Medium** – between 50 and 250 employees.
Sales operation	This refers to everyone who works as part of the sales department. It would include support and service related staff. A sales team relates more to people involved in the day-to-day activity of selling.
Sales Executive	The person who actually does the day-to-day selling of your products or services. Someone could also be referred to as an Account Manager, Account Director, etc.
Customer	A company or individual who is currently buying your *products* or who has done in the recent past. (To simplify the difference between a customer and a client we will use the term 'customer' throughout the book).
Client	Someone who is currently buying your *services* or who has done in the recent past.
Target account	A company that you have no business with but are planning to in the future.
USPs	Unique Selling Points. Areas where your company has an edge or something different to your competitors and where value can be added.

Sales term	Meaning
Mailshot	An introduction letter or leaflet which can be sent out as part of a marketing campaign.
eShot	An introduction email which can be sent out as part of a marketing campaign.
SEO	Search Engine Optimisation. Improving the visibility of a company's website or a web page on Internet search engines.
KPIs	Key Performance Indicators. They can be used as part of the sales performance measurement process. This can apply to sales, operational and strategic goals.
PDP	A Personal Development Plan can be used as part of the appraisal process.
HR	A Human Resources department is responsible for policies and procedures in relation to managing people. This can also include interviewing, helping to manage disputes, progress and development plans and disciplinary action.

Chapter 1
Responding to changes in the market

Chapter 1
Responding to changes in the market

This chapter considers a number of factors which can affect how well business owners respond to change, much of which you can influence. This includes:

- **Identifying economic and market influences.**
- **Adapting a company's sales culture.**

It looks at how external changes to the economic environment and the market can affect a company. It also examines how you can identify changes which you may feel are outside of your control.

The chapter will examine how you can respond to these challenges, partly by developing an appropriate sales culture. Finally it will look at ways in which you see and deal with particular issues. This can then be used to improve your leadership and management skills.

Identifying economic and market influences

There are two important external issues an SME sales operation will face. These are changes that can occur in the economy and the market you operate in.

By examining these areas you will be able to identify opportunities and threats, which can then be used as part of your planning processes. If these areas are assessed correctly and then acted upon, you will be in a better position to deal with them.

Economic changes

Business performance is affected by the economy. This is why it is important to factor changes in economic trends into your sales plans and targets. Economists have shown that the performance of an economy tends to work through a cycle.

Before explaining how you can use this information to help you improve performance, it can be a useful reminder to describe three familiar economic trends:

1. **Boom** – If an economy grows quickly, a boom can follow with high levels of sales and investment by companies, consumers and the government. A boom can lead to prosperity but also over-confidence in the business community and too much borrowing, which in turn can lead to an economic downturn.

2. **Downturn** – In an economic downturn, incomes and output start to fall. Rising costs of labour (and materials) increases the costs of products and services. This will eat into profits, putting smaller companies under pressure. It can cause downsizing and restructuring in order to adapt to the new conditions.

3. **Recovery and upturn** – As the economy recovers from a downturn, a company's revenues are more likely to increase, leading to growth. Consumers generally start to spend more as they are more confident in the security of their employment.

It is essential that your sales plans and targets accurately reflect the stage that the current economic cycle is in and the likely direction the economy is heading in. However, this can sometimes be hard to predict, as we have seen, economic events can affect companies in terms of supply and demand and bank lending.

A typical business cycle can be shown graphically, see the diagram below. It was first identified in the nineteenth century by Dunoyer and it compares economic growth over time in relation to boom, downturn, recovery and upturn.

ECONOMIC CYCLE

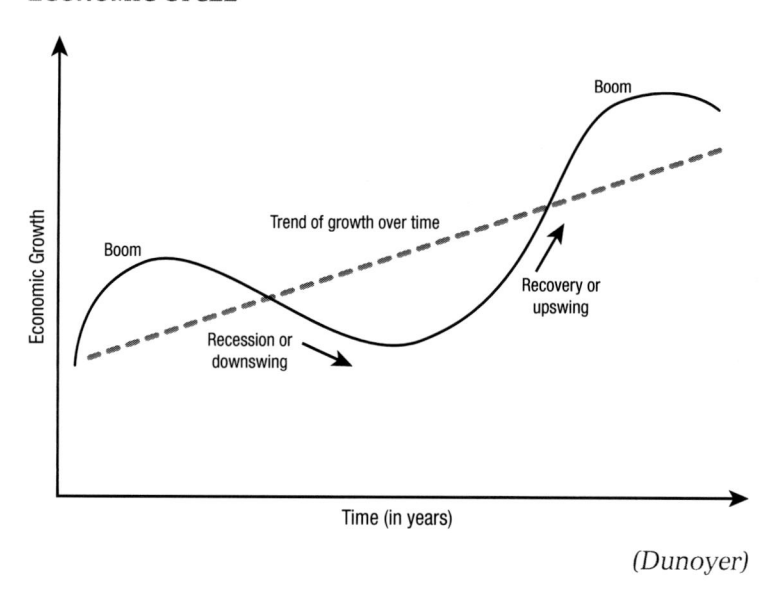

(Dunoyer)

How does this cycle affect my company?

It is clear that this economic cycle can have a major influence on the performance of a small or medium-sized company (i.e. SMEs). As an economy moves from one stage of the cycle to another there are changes in trading conditions. However, not all companies are equally affected and not all are pro-active in looking at different ways to improve their sales performance.

Some companies, for example the producers or retailers of essential items such as basic foodstuffs, may notice little change in demand for their products over time. This is because the items they sell are ones which consumers feel the need to purchase even when incomes are falling.

Demand for these products is not as sensitive to changes in income. But for other products and services, prices can be more sensitive to changes in income levels, and they will react more sharply to the stages of the economic cycle.

Similarly, in an economic downturn, online resellers might find that more customers use their services. This could be because they are lower in price than many high street retailers, as their overheads are lower.

All of these factors help to explain why it is important to understand the current position of the economy and the effect it can have on your company.

Economic indicators

By selecting the main economic indicators that can affect trading conditions, business owners can make a useful first step in trying to anticipate future conditions in their marketplace. Indicators could include:

- Interest and exchange rates.

- The level of inflation.
- Unemployment.
- The rise in overall bankruptcies.
- The number of new business start-ups and closures.
- Bank lending and government borrowing figures.
- The strength of the UK and world economy.

It is the change in these external indicators that present clues as to the future performance of the economy. By regularly assessing this type of information in a structured manner, you may be able to assess what strategies to take to create opportunities for your company. The following exercise gives you some practical steps to follow:

EXERCISE

	Economic Indicators
1.	Look at each economic indicator in turn and gather information which accurately reflects the current position.
2.	Compare this to the position 2 – 3 years ago.
3.	From current economic forecasts, think about the likely future position of the national, European and world economy and then consider how these conditions will affect you.

Market changes

Changes will also be taking place in the market you operate in. If companies do not adapt, they risk missing revenue opportunities or incurring diminishing returns from their sales and marketing efforts. If a response to the external environment is left too long, valuable sales opportunities can also be missed.

PRACTICAL POINTER

Companies who can adapt quickly to changes in their marketplace will have more chance of gaining a competitive advantage.

Adapting to change is often a key determinant of continued success. A good example of this in recent years has been the introduction of new technology. The Internet continues to have a major impact on how consumers and companies buy and sell products.

One of the key decisions for many SME's today is to decide what needs to be sold directly and what proportion could be sold online. Some companies who sell online might need to think about the balance between the revenue generated from this method compared to that produced by a direct sales team.

Johnson (1992) designed a useful three-stage model (which he called *Strategic Drift*), which can be adapted to help companies with this type of decision. It can be used to examine the market and to compare your current position to a likely future position. Johnson's model works in the following way:

STAGE ONE

This is where small, incremental changes that might go unnoticed take place in a market. No initial actions are taken. If sales revenues start to be affected, more rigorous managerial controls will be needed to address this. For example, managers may focus more on targeting and sales activity. This might solve some sales issues but much will also depend on the trend in the current market as well as how well the company is currently performing.

STAGE TWO

If a change in the market continues to take place, it will often lead to a traumatic period for business owners. There may be alterations of personnel, both at a senior management level and within a sales team, as companies attempt to recover from poor sales or lost revenue. Different strategies might be tried to 'fix' the problem as morale may decline if nothing is done.

STAGE THREE

A company recognises the severity of the market changes and realises that they will need to make a dramatic strategic shift to increase revenues, profits and market share. This can be challenging even if it is successful, especially if lost revenues are not recovered or sales growth is slow.

These stages can be illustrated in a way that can help business owners review their position relative to the sales targets. The following diagram, Johnson's risk of *Strategic Drift*, compares the amount of change over time during the three stages.

RISK OF STRATEGIC DRIFT

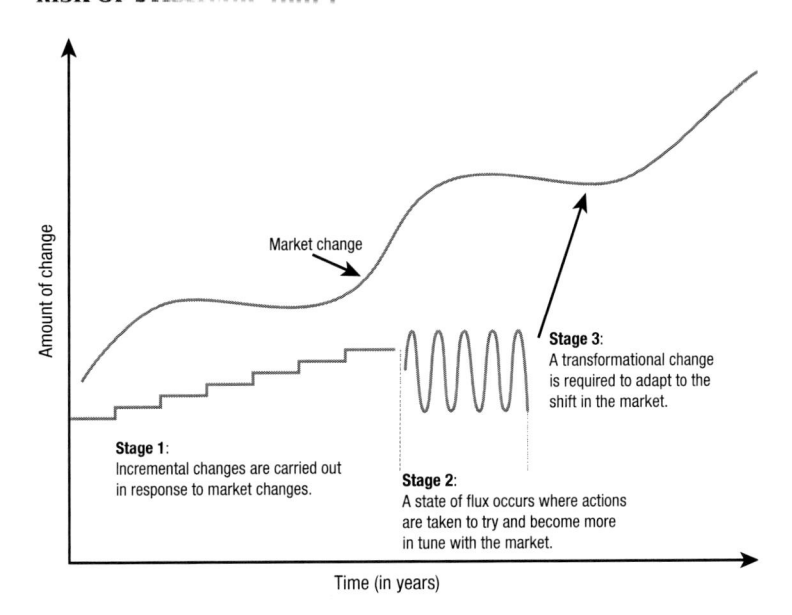

Amount of change (y-axis) vs **Time (in years)** (x-axis)

- Market change
- **Stage 1:** Incremental changes are carried out in response to market changes.
- **Stage 2:** A state of flux occurs where actions are taken to try and become more in tune with the market.
- **Stage 3:** A transformational change is required to adapt to the shift in the market.

(Johnson 1992)

You need to be aware of the risk of drifting away from your current position in the market you compete in. Once this has been established you can examine where you are relative to the ideal position.

Moving on from this; identifying your ideal position can be even more challenging. Using an adaptation of *Mercer's Position Map* (1996) you will be able to compare your current position relative to your ideal perceived position. It is then possible to identify what changes you might need to make in order to increase revenue and profit margins.

The *Position Map* can also help to show if your market is moving towards a commodity-type sale or not. It compares the following elements, for example:

1. Whether a product or service might better be sold on the Internet or through an indirect sales channel.
2. Whether the product or service is seen as a commodity or higher value sale.

The following diagram illustrates a company's current market position compared to where it would like to be. The existing position shown as the 'old ideal' has a focus on the Internet (i.e. technology based selling) and is commodity based (i.e. lower cost). In this example, it will be replaced with a new ideal position of direct selling and higher value focus.

POSITION MAP

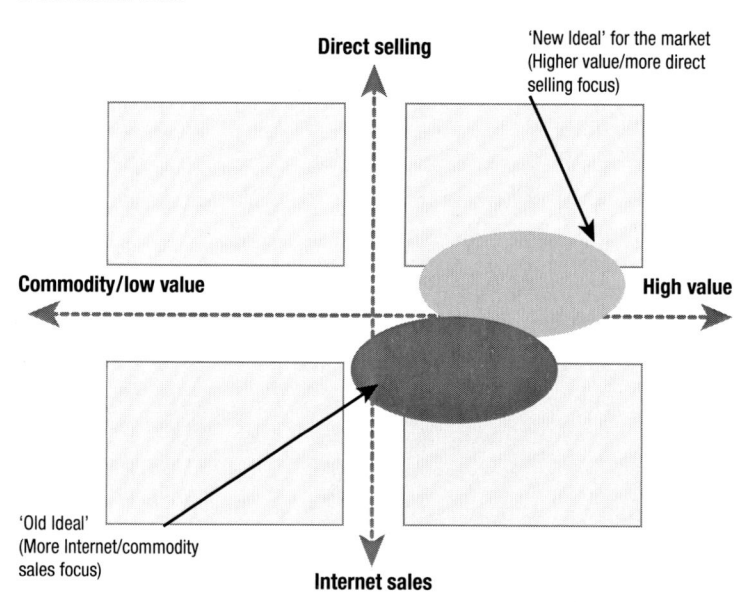

(Mercer 1996)

This shift will represent a new challenge because of the change in sales focus. It might result in adapting your sales strategy in order to gain new market share to achieve growth. There are some practical steps that you can use to compare your existing and ideal positions in order to create your own *Position Map*. As an example, work through the following exercise:

EXERCISE

	Marketing Changes Creating your own *Position Map*
1.	Pick two key areas intended for market changes. For example, the axis in the *Position Map* above has been chosen to reflect the impact of new technology.
2.	Think about how you sell your products and services in relation to different issues you may be facing.
3.	Plot the current position which you feel your company occupies.
4.	Identify the ideal future position you would like to occupy.
5.	Look at what strategy and actions need to be taken to move towards your 'ideal' market position.

By regularly examining the needs of your customers (which can change over time), you can ensure that their requirements are understood. You can undertake market research to adapt to changes in your market. This will help you to develop your own sales and marketing strategy. This is covered in more detail in Chapter 2, *Creating a sales and marketing strategy*.

Scenario Planning

Another practical way of looking at how you can adapt to change by using good business development techniques is through a process called *Scenario Planning*. This has been used successfully for a number of years. During the 1970s, Wack and Newland developed ways to help managers change how they see different business situations.

Scenario planning allows you to have an objective approach to changes in market conditions by considering areas which can sometimes be neglected. It will help you understand what your company's future could look like from a different viewpoint. To help with this, consider following these practical steps:

EXERCISE

	Scenario Planning
1.	Brainstorm with colleagues what you consider to be the most important economic and market issues you face.
2.	Select five issues which you think are the most important and gather relevant information on each.
3.	Prioritise these issues by giving them a score between 1 and 5 (a score of 1 being a low priority; and a score of 5 being a high priority).
4.	Score each issue on the likelihood of it occurring (i.e. a score of 1 being very unlikely; and a score of 5 being very likely), and then multiply this by the priority score.
5.	Look at what actions are required to address this.

The issues that you uncover from this activity can be rated on their potential impact and the likelihood of them happening. Once you have identified the issues which have the biggest impact they can be illustrated as follows:

Scenario Planning

Issue One	Increase in revenue due to improving economic conditions
Priority of the issue	1 2 3 (4) 5
Likelihood of it occurring	1 2 3 4 (5)
Priority multiplied by likelihood	4 X 5 = 20

Note. The score from the above activity means that this issue is an important one (as it is 20 out of a possible maximum of 25). This could have a high likelihood of occurring if economic conditions stay as they are for a period of time. This will improve the quality of your sales strategy and help you to plan more effectively.

PRACTICAL POINTER

You can reduce some aspects of uncertainty in your long-term planning by constructing different scenarios to explore possible outcomes and consequences.

In order to respond to changes in the economy and in your market, you need to think about situations and their effect on your company. By taking time to review this, you are better placed to anticipate changes and to respond to them more quickly than your competitors. You will then need to provide plans to enable your sales operation to respond to the challenges involved.

Adapting a company's sales culture

You are unlikely to be able to control changes in market conditions, but you can decide how to respond to them. This can be influenced by looking at the type of sales culture your company has. There are important areas within your control, including:

- The working environment and your company's values.
- Your sales culture and the unspoken Psychological Contract (Robinson and Rousseau, 1994), which exists between an employer and employee.
- Being solution-focused when adapting to change.

All three areas are important to consider if business opportunities are to be maximised.

The working environment

Motivational benefits can be obtained by a sales team if they feel they can use their initiative and develop as individuals. Working in an environment which supports trust allows employees to pull together even if there are differences in character and experiences.

A dilemma for many business owners is whether to manage a sales team directly or to delegate this to a dedicated sales manager. Whoever has overall control of a sales team must allow some degree of freedom within the team while still maintaining overall control over their daily routines. This can be done by giving feedback and encouragement to members of the team in order to progress towards clear strategic goals.

By defining these goals in terms of your sales objectives and targets, and by measuring them, they will be easier to meet.

Company values

Kanter (1997) said that shared values may contribute to holding a company together; in which case, business owners should think about the impact of not considering the views of employees in their sales operation. By ignoring or preventing relevant views and ideas from surfacing, business owners may distance themselves from key sales issues. This can then lead to a barrier developing between sales executives and customers, causing missed opportunities.

Asking for constructive opinions can promote discussion, which can be useful when appraising members of a sales team because it ensures their ideas are acknowledged.

It is important to develop some of the ideas coming from your sales operation by:

- Having a collaborative management style.
- Looking for business solutions (including areas which might contradict your own views).
- Using internal processes to help maintain objectivity.

These issues can affect the quality of your progress, so adhering to them will help you to maintain the right perspective.

PRACTICAL POINTER

Often, a business owner's leadership and management skills are key factors in relation to people feeling in control of their job roles.

Involving key members of your sales team in some parts of the decision-making process can be achieved by inviting positive contributions and delegating certain tasks. It is a worthwhile exercise to review the key business objectives of your company to ensure that the common goals are at the centre of any discussions.

By involving people, allowing them to speak honestly and, at times, question the existing strategy, you will also show an open approach.

Your sales culture

Any working environment will benefit from a 'high performance culture'. Every company is unique in some way and individual views often differ, so it is useful to consider what elements or different groups work well together. This will help to build a positive culture.

However, a sales culture is made up of a variety of elements, which can prove difficult to change. Johnson (1988) developed a useful model called *The Cultural Web*, which helps SMEs consider these different elements. This allows you to break them down and to adapt them piece by piece. These elements are:

- Stories of past experiences and successes.
- Symbols (i.e. visual representations of the company).
- The power structure in the organisation.
- Rituals and routines.

- Organisational structures.
- Control systems.

THE CULTURAL WEB

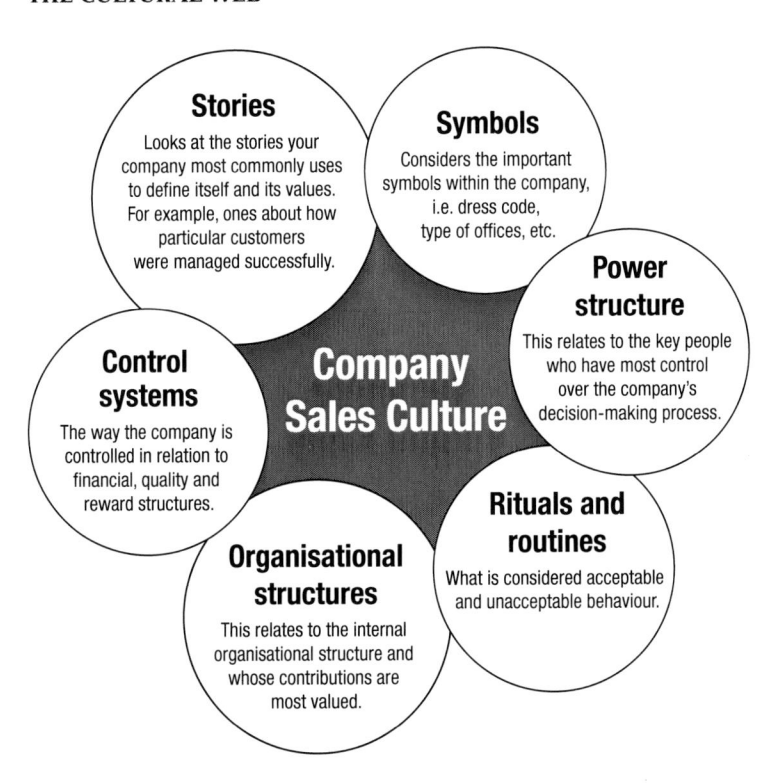

Stories
Looks at the stories your company most commonly uses to define itself and its values. For example, ones about how particular customers were managed successfully.

Symbols
Considers the important symbols within the company, i.e. dress code, type of offices, etc.

Power structure
This relates to the key people who have most control over the company's decision-making process.

Control systems
The way the company is controlled in relation to financial, quality and reward structures.

Company Sales Culture

Rituals and routines
What is considered acceptable and unacceptable behaviour.

Organisational structures
This relates to the internal organisational structure and whose contributions are most valued.

(Johnson 1988)

You can plan how to change your own sales culture from where it is to where you would like it to be by using the following steps:

EXERCISE

	Your Sales Culture
1.	Take each of the elements in turn and define their characteristics.
2.	Compare these to where you would like to be in each area and plan how to achieve this.
3.	Discuss this with relevant colleagues and be prepared to adapt your ideas.
4.	Communicate and implement any changes sensitively to avoid misunderstandings and resistance.

By separating out each element using Johnson's *Cultural Web*, changes can be made to adapt your company culture in a progressive way. It also helps you to develop a positive cultural mindset. This can be a particularly useful exercise for a sales operation to go through, allowing you to consider the impact of any changes you make.

Your psychological contract

The Psychological Contract (Robinson and Rousseau 1994) is another useful model which explores the relationship between formal and informal company rules. It can be used to highlight contradictions between a sales executive's views of what he/she is expected to do at work (informal and unwritten) and your company policy (formal and documented). Some of these views might be implied rather than explicitly stated.

The strength of many 'rules and regulations' will often depend on how strictly they are administered and the willingness of a business owner to carry them out.

Mismatches can occur for new employees if the sales culture is different from what they were expecting. This can happen if what was communicated to them at their interview is different to the reality once they start in their job role.

By examining a company's culture, misunderstandings can be avoided, thereby improving performance and staff retention. Further benefits can be achieved if sales executives and managers feel empowered and are allowed to use their initiative in certain areas.

The Psychological Contract can be illustrated in the following way:

THE PSYCHOLOGICAL CONTRACT

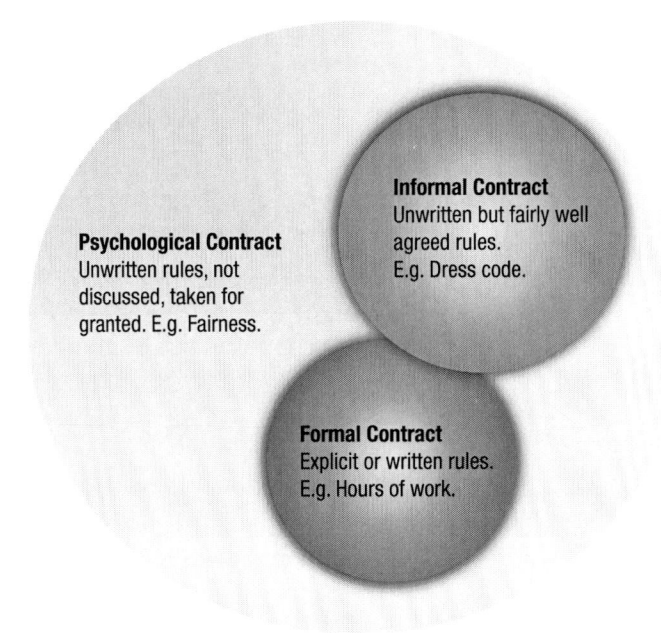

Psychological Contract
Unwritten rules, not discussed, taken for granted. E.g. Fairness.

Informal Contract
Unwritten but fairly well agreed rules.
E.g. Dress code.

Formal Contract
Explicit or written rules.
E.g. Hours of work.

(Robinson and Rousseau 1994)

Improved sales behaviour and performance can be achieved by breaking down barriers which may de-motivate sales executives. By working through the next activity you will be able to identify areas which might need to be clearly defined, for example:

EXERCISE

	Your Psychological Contract
1.	Take each of the following areas in turn: • The Psychological Contract. • The Informal Contract. • The Formal Contract. Ask your management team to give their ideas on each element. For example, what will motivate sales executives and what could be taken for granted?
2.	Discuss what types of behaviour are expected but not clearly stated or managed.
3.	• Use this information to establish whether there are any areas which need to be made more explicit. • Are any additional meetings needed in order to make guidelines clearer? • Find out if there are any existing procedures which are perceived as unfair or could be improved.

The Psychological Contract can be compared to a set of perceptions held in the minds of individuals. Some expectations might be obvious and don't need stating. Members of a sales team may not be aware of their expectations until a breach occurs and rules are broken.

It is useful to get feedback about your company culture from existing members of your sales operation. This can be done through a progress and development review. You should also allow people who leave the company to give feedback. You can do this by using 'exit' interviews from employees, asking them about their initial impression upon joining and the impression they have before they leave. This can then be compared and action taken as required, ensuring that you learn from it.

If you follow this process you need to be objective in order to get the most out of it.

Being solution focused

Some challenges and company issues do not just happen; we might create them (directly or indirectly). As a business owner if you think an issue has been caused by internal circumstances, the solution could be more to do with:

- Changing the situation.
- Changing your own perception (or someone else's)!
- Learning to live with the situation.

You can adopt different approaches to solve these issues. For example:

1. LET THEM HAPPEN

Not all issues need solving; sometimes they will solve themselves over time. Some things are better left alone. Think about whether the solution makes the problem worth solving!

2. MAKE IT HAPPEN

Try to tackle the issue in a way that brings it out in the open.

3. HELP IT TO HAPPEN

This is somewhere between the two and involves a mixture of control and encouragement (and a decision on whether to be pro-active or reactive).

Business owners often feel the need to 'make things happen'. There can be a natural tendency to want to solve an issue or be in control. Some issues can be complex with strong connections to others. By prioritising, you can tackle the important issues first or look at whether to review a situation in the future. Whatever your management style, you need to be consistent when looking at how you can improve your decision-making processes.

Have an objective and patient approach to solving issues and take the time to review any changes you make to ensure that they work effectively. This will mean that ideas are well defined and that any suggestions for solving a particular issue are properly explored. The following ten steps can help to develop these skills and is based on advice known as *Precepts* by Martin (2000).

EXERCISE

	Solving issues
1.	Challenge yourself, any fixed ideas and mindsets.
2.	Take the time to see something from another person's point of view.
3.	Summarise issues rather than look at each one in great detail. This makes them easier to understand and communicate to others.
4.	Don't be afraid of discussing an issue and trying to see a situation from different perspectives.
5.	Build up, don't knock down! Be positive about developing ideas you are building (or an idea someone else has)!
6.	Live with some degree of ambiguity. People can often be too concerned if things aren't always clear.
7.	Encourage and nurture creativity, it can often help to solve certain issues.
8.	Involve other people, where appropriate, in order to get new ideas.
9.	Avoid rejecting ideas too early as part of your decision-making process.
10.	Think about what you want and make sure that any outcomes you agree are managed.

Don't forget that although our minds can store vast amounts of information we can only think about a small amount at any one time. Miller (1956) stated that we can, on average, remember seven chunks of information simultaneously. That is why you should formalise any issues you are looking to solve and then agree timeframes for doing so.

In order to make use of these concepts, ask yourself the following questions:

- What is the state of the economy your company is performing in at present?
- What type of market position are you currently in and is it ideal or not?
- Is your sales culture consistent with your sales challenges?
- Are employee's expectations in line with what the company offers?

By considering these areas you can start to make changes to your sales operation and other parts of your company's structure. These will help you to have an effective sales culture to support your company goals.

Other ways of dealing with sales challenges and solving issues are looked at in more detail in Chapter 6, *A strategy to manage different types of people,* in the section, *Overcoming different sales challenges.*

Chapter summary

This chapter covered two main areas:

- Identifying economic and market influences.
- Adapting a company's sales culture.

Economic and market influences affect sales performance and involve thinking about where you are currently in terms of market position and where you would like to be. This needs to be put directly into your sales strategy and business processes.

From this, build a sales culture which reflects the aspirations you have in your market sector. By doing this and involving people in the process, you increase your chances of developing a constructive plan which you can implement.

Key points

✓ Take the time to look at any changes in the economy and your market that could affect you.

✓ Think about what the ideal position for your company is by considering different scenarios for the future.

✓ Review the elements which make up your sales culture, i.e. the relationship between individual members of a sales team and the company's objectives.

✓ Look at different ways to solve issues by involving relevant people in order to establish the positive outcomes you want.

Chapter 2
Creating a sales and marketing strategy

Chapter 2
Creating a sales and marketing strategy

For every business owner, effective marketing can grow sales revenue and improve the chances of your products and services increasing their market share. To help you, this chapter will look at:

- **Defining your marketing objectives.**
- **Analysing your sales performance.**
- **Effective branding.**

It will explain the importance of having a clear marketing strategy and strong link to sales. It will challenge you about the need to have a marketing budget and, if you don't have one, why you should consider creating one. It will consider what marketing objectives to use to enable you to improve your sales performance.

The chapter also considers how to make sense of your sales data by looking at trends to manage future marketing initiatives more effectively. It analyses how your potential customers make their buying decisions, giving you the opportunity to influence them. Finally, it covers branding which will help you co-ordinate your marketing activities to give you the best chance of promoting your products and services effectively.

Defining your marketing objectives

Having a mission statement

Before you think about defining the objectives of your marketing strategy, consider what it actually is that your company stands for. This relates to its vision and values.

Having a vision is important as it helps to define what your marketing strategy will look like. Métayer (2004) defined vision as a combination of three elements:

- A company's fundamental reason for existence beyond just making profits.
- Its core values.
- Its ambitions and plans for its own future.

As a business owner, your vision has important implications for your sales operation as well as for your systems and processes. It helps to set the standard by which you can measure your progress.

The first steps needed to achieve this are to define your vision and principals by producing a *Mission Statement*. If you have not already created one, complete the following sentences:

EXERCISE

	Mission Statement
1.	We exist to:
2.	Our core values are:
3.	We want to achieve:

By listing your core values it will make it easier to link this to your sales and marketing strategy. You should consider putting your *Mission Statement* on your website to reinforce your commitment to these values.

Once the aims of the company are defined you can consider what data and information is needed by a sales team to be effective and the ways in which they can obtain and share it.

Creating a marketing strategy

Sales and marketing are often talked about in the same way, but although they are linked, there are some significant differences! Selling involves persuading a potential customer to buy something through direct or indirect channels. Marketing refers more to how you brand and promote your products and services. Many SMEs don't see the need to have a marketing strategy or a separate budget for one. However, good marketing can help you sell more, especially if you closely align it to a sales strategy. Before you think about how you are going to plan for the next quarter, year and beyond, think about the type of marketing you need. This involves knowing the outcomes you are looking for and the actions involved in achieving them.

Many business owners will be familiar with the term *management by objectives* as part of the way in which the stated aims of the company should be managed. In order to create the first steps for your own marketing strategy you need to think about:

1. The types of objectives you have; these should involve goals and should be adaptable to change. They need to reflect the state of the economy, your market and the type of sales culture you have. (This was covered in Chapter 1, *Responding to changes in the market.*)

2. Understanding your customer – It is important to think about what the customer wants first, rather than what products or services you sell! By focusing on their needs you will be in a better position to think about what type of strategy to adopt to meet them.

A marketing strategy also involves thinking about what approach to use in order to achieve your objectives, e.g. ways to sell your products or services differently in the future or to target another market.

An effective marketing strategy will take time to formulate and will need resources to implement it. It will involve senior management's drive and other relevant colleagues' 'buy in' to see it through. Your employees need to believe in the process to avoid any potential resistance to it! If you do introduce changes, think about how quickly to do this in order to give people a chance to accept them.

Any change process should be realistic and achievable in order for it to be successful. A summary of how to develop a strategy is often easier to articulate if you write down your objectives that could, for example, be to:

1. Understand your target accounts and customers' needs.
2. Develop marketing objectives aligned with sales objectives.
3. Carry out the plans you need to put in place. This is covered in Chapter 3, *Implementing your strategy (with a sales operations plan)*.

Complete the exercise below. It will help you to define your marketing objectives.

EXERCISE

	Your current business aims List three key business objectives and when they should be achieved
1.	
2.	
3.	

By knowing what you are aiming for with your business goals, you make it easier to think about how your products and services can be marketed. You should also consider the budget or percentage of revenue 'spend' you want to allocate to this.

As part of your marketing strategy you will probably already use some essential marketing tools to promote your business. As well as a website you will no doubt have considered other forms of promotion through:

- Advertising (radio, magazine, newspaper).
- Mailshot/eShot – directly (or with a lead generation company).
- The Internet – Search Engine Optimisation (SEO).
- Local business and national trade associations.

- Business directories.
- Marketing collateral/brochures.
- Business seminars and networking events.
- Direct sales.

Some of the above can be achieved with a relatively small budget; for example, writing case studies in relation to customers who have been satisfied with your products and services. These will support your marketing by acting as a form of proof statement. This can be included on your website or sent out as part of a marketing campaign.

It is a good way of communicating to your target audience about the value you can add. It also gives them an insight into your company's ability to understand how to meet a customer's needs.

Marketing objectives typically revolve around increasing market share in an existing market or developing into a new market segment. This section will explore these areas so that you can think about what type of marketing strategy would be best for you.

Porter's Generic Strategies (1980) presented a distinct choice as to whether to promote a low cost product/service, or a differentiated one. The key aspect to this is to avoid falling between these two positions as potential customers can become confused by this type of market positioning.

Customers are often prepared to spend more on the additional value presented by a differentiated product or service. If they are not, then either this value hasn't been totally understood or their main focus is often based around the price. This could be because they perceive the value can still be achieved at a lower price cost, or they might not want to pay for any perceived value!

This can be illustrated with an example of a particular tactic which supports this type of strategy:

GENERIC STRATEGIES

Low cost ⬅ **PRODUCT/SERVICE** ➡ **Uniqueness**

COST LEADERSHIP Strategy	**DIFFERENTIATION Strategy**
Tactic: Promote a cost advantage over your competitors.	Tactic: Promote a distinctive brand image to add value.
This is often a commodity product or service focusing on being the cheapest, i.e. why look somewhere else when we won't be beaten on price!	This is often a product or service which is higher in price and looks to justify the extra value, i.e. why look somewhere else when the value you need is here!

(Porter 1980)

Once you are clear about which of the above strategies is more suitable for you, marketing activities and promotion become easier to implement. There can be times when you might choose a different strategy for different products and services. Much will depend on what you sell and the positioning strategy you have. However, other factors such as the state of the market will also have an impact on how successful your strategy is.

One trap to avoid is to think that you have a differentiation strategy only to find that you are regularly losing sales based on price! In order to ensure that this doesn't happen, look more closely at how you are selling and marketing your products and services. This will help you isolate any potential issues.

Another approach to help overcome this is to look at maintaining or growing market share through two options, as defined by Ansoff (1957):

1. **Market Penetration** – Sell more of the same product or service to existing customers in an existing marketplace.
2. **Market Development** – Sell existing products or services into new markets.

This framework enables you to think about the tactics to adopt in order to achieve your marketing objectives. If you decide upon a *Market Penetration* strategy you should use promotions to incentivise existing customers to buy more, such as loyalty schemes. If you choose a *Market Development* strategy you might look at new sales channels to attract new prospects.

ANSOFF'S MATRIX

Existing ⬅ MARKET ➡ New

Market PENETRATION	Market DEVELOPMENT
Tactics include: Giving customers a larger range of buying options.	Tactics include: Building relationships in new segments to market your existing products and services.

(Ansoff 1957)

These two areas are good starting points when pricing and promoting your products and services.

EXERCISE

In order to develop this, consider the following two questions:

	Developing your Marketing Strategy
1.	Are you promoting a low cost (commodity) or differentiation (value) proposition?
2.	Is your main focus to develop your existing market further or establish different positioning (and/or new markets)?

Think about the consequences of your answers and whether they meet your objectives.

The next step is to look at the type of information you need to support your marketing strategy and campaigns. A part of this is to make sense of any marketing data you have to ensure that your business aims are achievable. To do this you first need to look at your sales performance.

Analysing your sales performance

Identifying and understanding sales trends

Making a correlation between different types of sales data can help you understand and manage your sales performance and the marketing resource needed to support it. For example, if you know that spending more on advertising in a particular area leads to increased sales; it makes sense to do so.

This can be developed further by identifying trends from your market research. A useful way to categorise sales information is to split it into quantitative and qualitative data. Quantitative data refers to statistics that make it easier to make sense of sales, whereas qualitative data includes people's view and ideas and is more subjective. With quantitative data, look for possible trends and cyclical fluctuations in order to predict sales outcomes.

There can also be other factors to consider; for example, your business might be seasonal or your market might have become mature. These are both factors which you will need to consider in relation to identifying trends.

The fictional monthly sales figures below will help you to consider trends:

ACTUAL MONTHLY SALES

Month	Sales in 000's	Month	Sales in 000's
January	9	July	9
February	12	August	18
March	15	September	21
April	15	October	24
May	18	November	12
June	21	December	24

In their present form it is difficult to make any real sense of these figures when trying to identify trends. In order to overcome this we need more analysis of the information. Look at the following table which gives a typical number of units sold per month for a particular product:

IDENTIFYING A TREND LINE

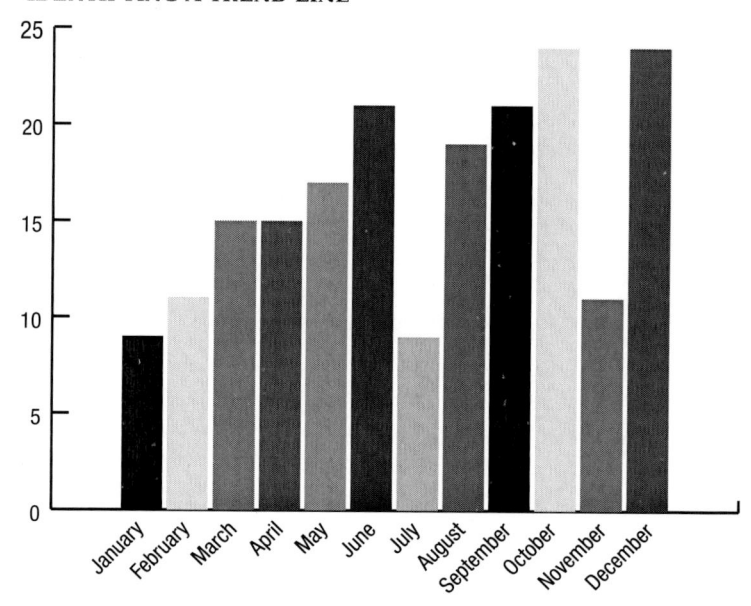

This bar chart takes the same data and illustrates it in a slightly different way, but it is still difficult to predict a trend. The trend seems upwards but there are fluctuations. How can you draw meaningful conclusions from this?

If you complete a three month *'moving average'* it will become much easier to see if any trend is taking place which can help to predict future sales. This technique involves using the sales figures for three months at a time and then dividing them by three. For example:

- January – 9,000
- February – 12,000
- March – 15,000

This gives a total of 36,000, which when divided by three tells us that 12,000 units are sold as an average for that period.

Place the period average result of 12,000 in the middle of the time period selected, in this case February (for the three months January – March); then take February, March and April and complete the same process (i.e. until all the data has been grouped into 3 month periods and divided by three.

This gives us a set of numbers that can help smooth out the data. January and December are excluded because they rely on sales data from the preceding and future months of a different year. The table below shows the moving averages created using the data in the previous *Actual Monthly Sales* table:

DATA CONVERTED INTO A THREE MONTH MOVING AVERAGE

Month	Sales 000's	Previous month, current month and next months' sales (000's)	3 month average (000's)
January	9	No data – we don't look at previous month because it is in another year.	Not applicable
February	12	(9+12+15)/3	12
March	15	(12+15+15)/3	14
April	15	(15+15+18)/3	16
May	18	(15+18+21)/3	18
June	21	(18+21+9)/3	16
July	9	(21+9+18)/3	16
August	18	(9+18+21)/3	16
September	21	(18+21+24)/3	21
October	24	(21+24+12)/3	19
November	12	(24+12+24)/3	20
December	24	No data – we don't look at the previous month because it is in another year.	Not applicable

By plotting these statistics into a bar chart, the peaks and troughs will be taken out. The trend can be converted into a *'trend line'* making it easier to predict current and future sales for marketing purposes.

USING MOVING AVERAGES TO SEE A TREND LINE

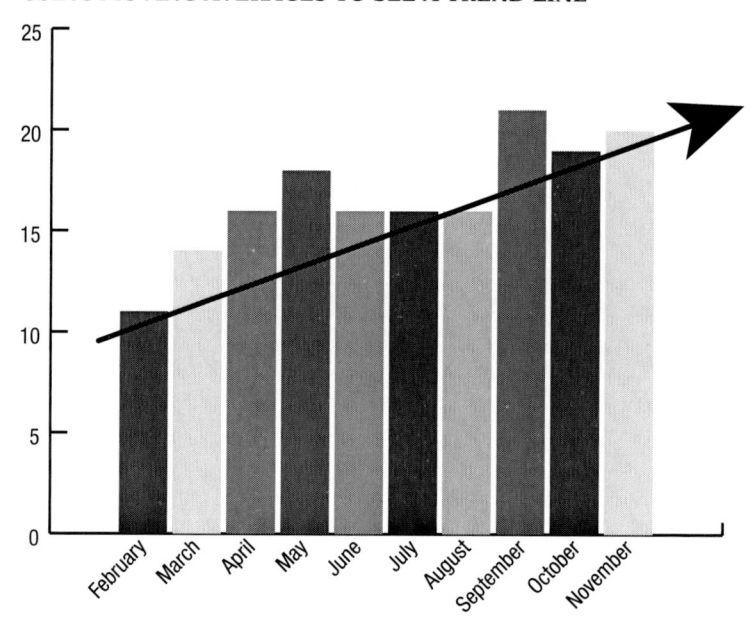

The data above the *'trend line'* implies that sales are likely to continue on an upward path in the following year (if current economic and market conditions prevail). This information can be used as one indicator to decide what marketing objectives and sales targets should be set for this product. But seasonal trends must be taken into account.

In order to relate this to your own products and services, complete the following exercise. It will help you understand the relationship between how much you spend on marketing and the sales you are achieving from this investment.

EXERCISE

	Making sense of marketing data
1.	Look at a marketing campaign and measure the level of response.
2.	Then take the data and see if there is a direct correlation between the investment on the campaign and the sales revenue generated.
3.	Use the moving average technique to smooth out any peaks and troughs to make any trend easier to see.
4.	Based on the information obtained, predict revenue for sales in twelve months time.
5.	Think about what other data would be helpful before committing to the target of market share you are looking for.

The purpose of these techniques is to identify trends in order to interpret your marketing data.

By using statistics like this you should have a clearer idea about the effectiveness of your marketing campaigns. It should also give you a good starting point to create realistic marketing objectives and strategies to achieve these objectives.

By looking at your sales trends you will be in a better position to plan what marketing you will need to do. Another area to look at which can help you to understand the strength of your selling proposition in the market place is branding.

Effective branding

A brand is really the identity of your product or service and how it relates to potential and existing customers. Brand associations include:

- Perceptions.
- Image.
- Identity.
- Beliefs.
- Attitudes.
- Feelings.

These associations illustrate why many people are loyal to a brand even if there isn't always a strong commercial reason to buy that product. This is why your brand image is a vital part of your sales and marketing strategy and why you should consider developing a brand identity for your products and services (although this section will refer to services as 'products' to provide a uniform terminology).

To achieve a brand identity, think about a term used by marketing specialists known as the *Marketing Mix* (Borden 1953). This was developed further by McCarthy (1960) who proposed a four part classification relating to:

- A company's **Product** (which can be service related).
- It's **Promotion**.
- The **Price** charged.
- The **Place** where the product can be purchased.

The following illustration is adapted from Borden's original:

THE MARKETING MIX

```
        PRODUCT  |  PROMOTION
                 |
        ─── The Marketing Mix ───
                 |
         PRICE   |   PLACE
```

The *Marketing Mix* is sometimes referred to as *The Four Ps*. Your selling proposition should be made up from these four elements by blending them together in a different way to your competitors to create *Unique Selling Points (USPs)*.

Although all four areas are important and the right balance between the elements is critical, for marketing purposes it could be argued that *Product* and *Promotion* are more associated with marketing. *Price* relates more to revenue generation, and profit and *Place* is more about an effective distribution chain/route to market. We will therefore focus more on product and promotion!

1. Product

How you market your products will depend on what type you sell and the target market you are trying to attract. *The Marketing Mix* will depend on whether you have a low cost (commodity) or differentiation strategy (as looked at earlier in this chapter). This can be affected by whether you sell directly to the consumer, through the Internet or business to business.

You will need to consider a number of factors when you design a product; for example, the brand name, quality, safety issues, support, etc (although not all of these will apply if your 'brand' is actually a service).

Two distinct elements attract customers to a product: the primary benefit that it brings, which is normally functional, i.e. what it does; and the emotional benefit someone gets from buying it, i.e. how it makes that person feel. The emotional benefit from buying a prestigious or well designed product will be higher than when buying commodity goods.

It is important to identify the primary and emotional benefits of your product in order to communicate them to your potential customers. Good customer service can also have a significant impact on a customer's perception of products.

EXERCISE

In relation to your own brand awareness, consider what you are selling in relation to your own products, for example:

Core and emotional benefits of your brand	
1.	What are the fundamental needs that your core product satisfies?
2.	What emotional benefits does this satisfy to someone who buys it?

This activity will help you decide what and how you promote your own products and services.

PRODUCT LIFE CYCLES

Up until now the focus has been on one single product. However, most companies supply more than one. You should consider the message you want to send for each product as well as that of your company. They are interlinked and should be used to reinforce each other.

If you are supplying a number of different products, consider the life cycle of each. Think about which will generate the sales revenue and profit needed for your company to grow. Each product will typically go through the same life cycle phase, although over differing time periods. If the customer fit is right it will achieve a growth in sales before tailing off, as the product life cycle matures. It finally declines as customers switch to more updated products/technology/services or new suppliers enter the market.

A typical cycle can be seen below:

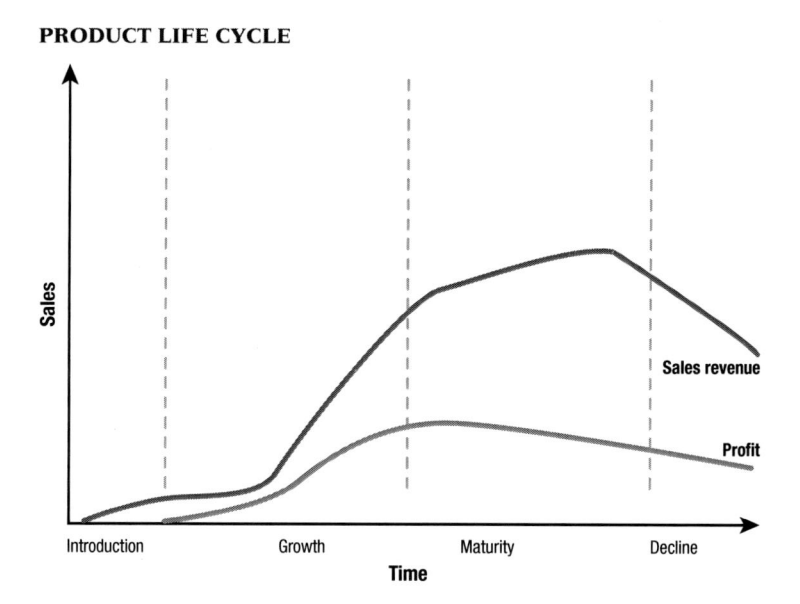

PRODUCT LIFE CYCLE

Y-axis: Sales
X-axis: Time — Introduction, Growth, Maturity, Decline
Curves: Sales revenue, Profit

Profits might take time to be achieved as initial investment costs need to be recovered. In a typical market they would be expected to rise and then fall over time as a market begins to mature. Much will depend on what stage you entered a market.

As the product is first introduced the focus is directed at creating consumer awareness in order to attract new customers. This may take a higher proportion of a marketing budget. As a market matures the focus of the campaign may change to retaining existing customers which should mean that less of a marketing budget is used for promotion.

Finding a balance on how much to spend on different products can be challenging. This is why an analysis of the products in relation to their demand is important. You will also want to assess product growth compared to overall market growth. This will help you to focus on the right areas and determine how to spend a marketing budget well.

In order to prioritise on different products in terms of marketing focus and budget spend, you should consider categorising them. This can be done by looking at your own market share as well as the growth of the market you are in, as illustrated using the 1968 *Boston Consulting Group (BCG) Matrix*. The four categories are:

1. **Stars** – High growth market, high market share. These are relatively new products which have a high market share in a growing market and require a high investment to keep up with or stay ahead of the competition.

2. **Cash cows** – Low growth market, high market share. These generate revenue and are established products. They have a large share of the market they are in, but the market itself is not growing. Their position needs to be managed and maintained but increased investment is unlikely as it won't produce more revenue easily.

3. **Dogs** – Low growth market, low market share. These are products which have a weak market share and low growth in the market they operate in. A decision should be made to agree whether to market them in the future.

4. **Question marks** – High growth market, low market share. These products pose a challenge as the market share needs to increase to justify them. A judgement needs to be made as to whether or not further investment is needed to achieve this.

The four categories can be illustrated in the following way:

THE BCG MATRIX

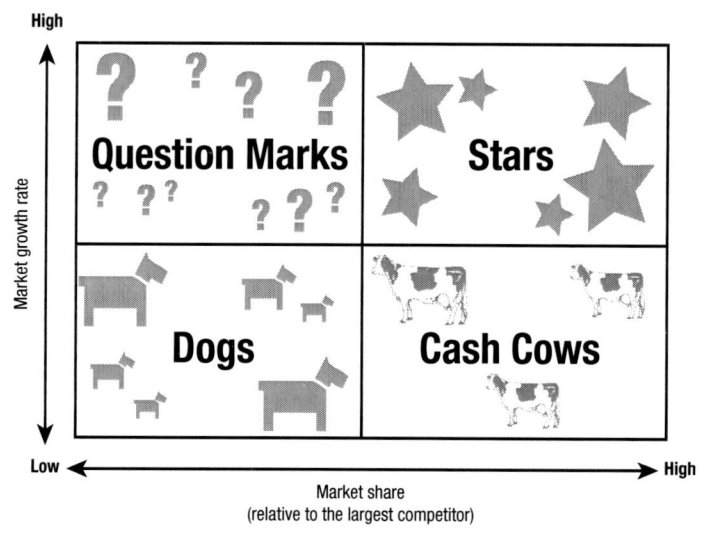

[A 2x2 matrix diagram with "Market growth rate" on the vertical axis (Low to High) and "Market share (relative to the largest competitor)" on the horizontal axis (Low to High). The four quadrants are: Question Marks (top-left), Stars (top-right), Dogs (bottom-left), Cash Cows (bottom-right).]

(Boston Consulting Group 1968)

Over time, the products change position: the 'ideal' movement would be starting as a *Question mark*, moving into a *Star* and then a *Cash Cow*. *Dogs* should be removed once their value deteriorates below a profitable level.

To help with this, complete the following exercise on product portfolio management. You will be able to analyse where each of your products are in their life cycle and you will need to either create a marketing budget or spend an existing one on a particular segment. This will allow you to review how effective your marketing spend is.

EXERCISE

	Product Portfolio Management
1.	What is the planned marketing expenditure for each of your products over the next 12 months?
2.	Place each of your current products into one of the four categories of the *BCG Matrix* and consider their relative market share and the growth potential of the market they are in.
3.	Does the proportion of the investment for each product reflect their position in the *Matrix*, (for example, are you investing in *Dogs* at the expense of *Stars*)?

By developing your own *BCG Matrix* you can look to avoid a common marketing mistake – the 'one size fits all' approach. Your marketing will be made more effective if you categorise your growth targets into different areas and then plan your marketing campaign accordingly.

We will now consider the next step in the *Marketing Mix*, promoting your products.

2. Promotion

In the context of the *Marketing Mix* there are four key steps to support the promotion of a product:

1. Establish who you are communicating your message to.
2. Define what you want the message to say.
3. Decide how you will convey this (mailshot/eShot, business magazine, radio, etc).

4. Review how successful your message has been and its impact on sales.

Decide whether you are targeting the consumer or business to business. You will also need to decide what level of contact you are targeting, i.e. a specialist, a director, middle management etc.

You need to consider how effective your marketing communication is in gaining the attention of your target audience and the percentage and quality of response you get from it. You may want to try different forms of promotion rather than just using one approach. This will depend on your budget and how successful a particular campaign is.

PRACTICAL POINTER

A co-ordinated marketing campaign, over an extended time period using a variety of methods, can have more impact than a 'one off' campaign.

When you decide on a particular marketing campaign, you should also consider your target audience. For example, a radio campaign is likely to be heard by a large number of people. The overall cost of this type of campaign is relatively high – even though the cost for each person who listens could be comparatively low and the campaign is likely to be listened to by people who you might not really want to target.

The following example highlights the cost for each person targeted, comparing four types of marketing campaign (rather than the total cost of a campaign).

COST VERSUS PERSONALISATION

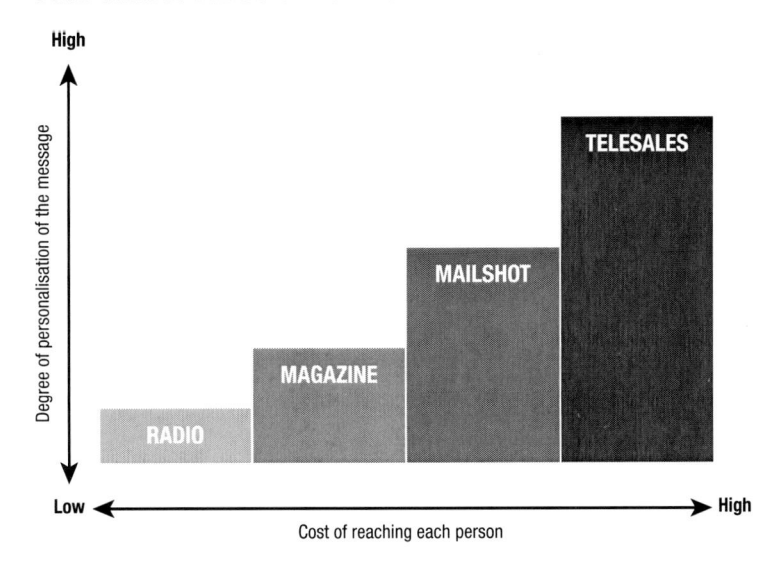

Chart: Degree of personalisation of the message (Low to High) vs Cost of reaching each person (Low to High), showing bars for RADIO, MAGAZINE, MAILSHOT, and TELESALES in ascending order.

A telesales campaign will reach significantly less people and therefore each contact will cost proportionately more. However, it is likely to be more personal and tailored. This means that you should consider the relationship between the quality of the message you want to send and the quantity of consumers/companies you want to target.

MEASURING THE SUCCESS OF A MARKETING CAMPAIGN

How effective your marketing campaign is will partly depend on how flexible you are. It may not be possible to make a sale from one advertisement or mailshot/eShot so your goal might be for a reactive campaign. This can happen when a potential customer looks at your website, possibly after some investment in a *Search Engine Optimisation (SEO)* campaign.

A useful method of measuring the success of your marketing campaigns is to focus on four key areas.

- Attention – Have you gained your target audience's attention?
- Interest – Have you created interest in your product?
- Desire – Has the campaign created a desire in your target audience?
- Action – Is there a reason for them to take action?

These points, which can be abbreviated in the acronym – A.I.D.A, were attributed to the advertising campaigner E. St. Elmo Lewis and are a useful reminder of what to focus on in relation to advertising.

The emphasis on each area could depend on the marketing investment you make. Once again if you are selling something of high value your focus is likely to be more on quality (with a differentiation strategy) or on how you meet a particular need or solve a particular issue. If you are selling a commodity product, the focus is likely to be more price-orientated. It is also important to consider the emotional element you might be hoping to communicate to your target audience (highlighted earlier) within the context of any campaign.

It is often the monitoring of a marketing campaign which will determine how successful your investment has been over time. For example, what percentage of companies targeted responded to you or engaged in a discussion or meeting with you?

One-off campaigns can see an increase in sales, but this can be short-lived and the levels of sales after the campaign often return back to where they were before you started.

It is a good idea to have marketing campaigns which follow on from each other, some of which might be seasonal. Each campaign should have a defined message, objectives and plan, and there should be an agreed timeframe between each one. If you are targetting a company you should decide whether to target a smaller number with a phone call, which takes time and is pro-active. Or you might decide to convey your message to a larger audience but without any follow-up.

Reactive campaigns will have a much lower percentage of success so you need to think about the type of strategy you want to follow and the effect each one might have. At the end of a campaign you should compare your pre-campaign expectation with what actually happened in terms of interest and, most importantly, in sales over time!

EXERCISE

You can review a marketing campaign using the following table:

	Promotion
1.	What was your marketing message?
2.	Who were the intended recipients of your message?
3.	How did you convey your message?
4.	Was it co-ordinated or did you focus on a single 'one off' communication?
5.	How many people (or target accounts) did you send it to?
6.	What was the cost for reaching each person (or target account)?
7.	What was your 'hit rate' percentage (that is the number of companies targeted divided by those that were interested)?
8.	What was the value of each sale gained (that is the revenue of additional sales minus the cost of the campaign)?

From this information you will be able to review the effectiveness of your marketing campaigns and evaluate the value from your investment.

The next part covers different ways to price your products.

3. Price

The relationship between price and value is important when setting the price of a product. This will involve internal financial considerations as well as sales and marketing elements as part of your strategy. You will need to consider your position in the market and factors like seasonal pricing, early payment discounts, recommended retail prices, etc.

A price also needs to reflect the value of a product or service, and premium prices are less likely to exist in a commodity market. Unless you are very well-known and have very high value brand awareness, potential customers are likely to make a comparison between your products and those of your competitors.

Even after a comparison is made they may remain with an existing supplier or delay a purchase. This can happen if a lower price has been offered by an existing supplier or if there is a guarantee of maintaining an existing product for a longer period rather than replacing it. This is particularly true in times of an economic downturn.

This is why it is important to make potential customers fully aware of exactly what is being offered and the real value of what you are selling. Key questions that you should ask in relation to price include:

WHAT DO THE COMPETITORS OFFER?

The availability and price of similar products by other suppliers are important factors to consider when setting your prices. Competitors may offer the same type and quality of product, or an alternative one, that achieves the same goal and satisfies a customer's need in the same way. This is why communicating your *USPs* in your marketing message will help you to distinguish yourself from your competitors.

WHAT IS THE COST OF BRINGING YOUR PRODUCT TO MARKET?

Many companies look at the total cost of making products and then add a certain percentage on. This should reflect market prices *and* the anticipated profit margins you expect to make.

You should break down the total costs of making a product into fixed and variable costs:

- **Fixed costs** are those that are fairly constant, regardless of how much or how little you sell (e.g. rental costs of a building, salaries).
- **Variable costs** are those that increase as your sales increase (e.g. additional staff costs, transport).

That is why when you are setting a price it must be higher than the variable cost, which will fluctuate.

WHAT IS THE CUSTOMER PREPARED TO PAY?

You will need to calculate prices in line with market prices. The demand for some products will vary significantly when the price is changed. This may depend on:

- Supply and demand of competing products.
- Tastes and fashion.
- The amount of a consumer's disposable income.

Products which enjoy high brand loyalty are not as responsive to a change in price and therefore a realistic price increase should mean that customers continue to purchase the product.

Another factor which can help determine your pricing is the type of customers you have and any new ones that you are targeting. Consider the following:

EXERCISE

	How are the prices set in your company?
1.	Have you examined the prices of your competitors, if so how?
2.	How is your pricing set, i.e. does it consider emotional as well as financial considerations for a buyer?
3.	What research have you done into how much your customers are willing to pay?

Pricing is a very important element of the *Marketing Mix* and needs careful planning and consideration. This leads on to the final part of the *Four P's*, which relates to getting your products to market.

4. Place

Place, or the distribution of a product, is concerned with how it is passed from the place of manufacture (if you actually make a product) to the customer. Considerations might include what distribution channel and inventory management system you use, order processing, transport, logistics, distribution, etc.

If your 'product' is actually a service then some of these steps won't be relevant, but getting the service to market will be! A service might also focus more on using the Internet via *Search Engine Optimisation (SEO)*.

There is a much shorter process from service provider to service user, but for a product there are more elements. For example, there are three levels of distribution which impact on the other elements of the *Marketing Mix*. This is shown in the diagram below which gives examples of how a producer can get a product to a consumer.

LEVELS OF DISTRIBUTION CHAIN

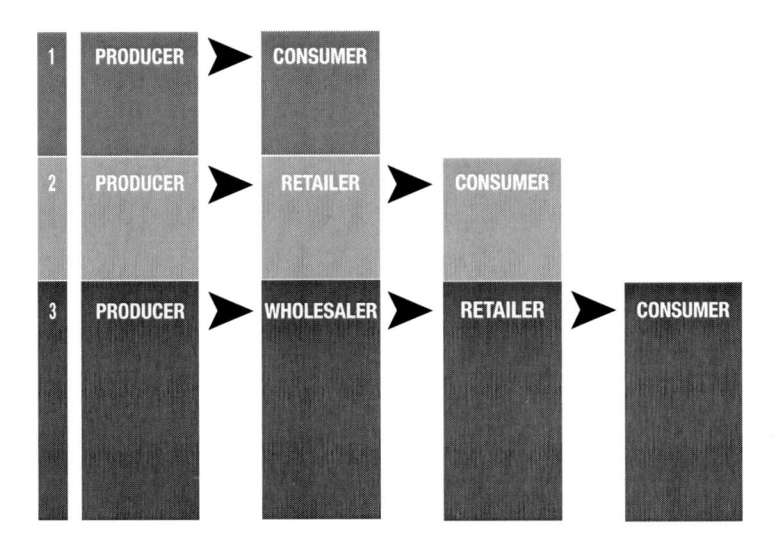

1	PRODUCER → CONSUMER
2	PRODUCER → RETAILER → CONSUMER
3	PRODUCER → WHOLESALER → RETAILER → CONSUMER

Some levels of distribution can be longer or shorter than others, depending on what processes are needed which relates to bringing your products to market.

If you sell an actual product, your strategy for distribution will depend on the nature of what you are supplying, whether you manufacture it and your current target market. For commodity products, the distribution channel is normally influenced by the need to generate sales and distribute the product to as wide a target market as possible.

More exclusive products tend to have fewer outlets. These outlets must reinforce the nature of the brand, i.e. a differentiation strategy. The choice of distribution channel will impact on all of the elements of the *Marketing Mix*. This may change as a product becomes better known, is replicated by a competitor or is commoditised, or as a market becomes mature.

It is important to establish whether you are targeting a specific segment within a market, multiple segments or coverage of the entire market. How these segments are divided can vary, but the key is to ensure that the definitions of your target market are clear and that the *Marketing Mix* is tailored to address them.

Finally, the longer the distribution process, the more chance there is that a customer can experience an issue of some kind, which they may link to your brand. This needs careful managing to ensure that the appropriate quality of distribution is delivered at each stage.

This section has explored the four elements of the *Marketing Mix*. Other factors like packaging, people and processes are also factors which can improve your focus when bringing a product to market. The *Marketing Mix concept* provides a useful framework which recognises that each element does not work in isolation. Used correctly, it will help you to implement your sales and marketing strategy.

Chapter summary

This chapter covered three main areas:

- Defining your marketing objectives.
- Analysing your sales performance.
- Effective branding.

We have looked at what it is that you stand for as a business owner and the values which are important to you. We have considered why it is necessary to have a marketing strategy which should involve a budget and be linked to your sales targets. We have also looked at how you can analyse your sales performance by considering the relationship between marketing data and customer buying decisions.

By getting your own *Marketing Mix* right you can tailor your campaigns to address your own target market. This will help you to deliver better results from any investment you make when marketing your products and services.

Key points

✓ Think about what sales and marketing strategy you want and the investment needed to implement it.

✓ Create a *Mission Statement* to provide the vision for your sales and marketing strategy.

✓ Analyse your sales trends and use this data to help you achieve your marketing objectives.

✓ Invest time to review your marketing activities and co-ordinate your efforts to build on each campaign.

✓ Ensure that you use all of the elements of the *Marketing Mix* to create your own unique selling proposition.

Chapter 3
Implementing your strategy
(with a sales operations plan)

Chapter 3
Implementing your strategy
(with a sales operations plan)

Companies often find that the saying 'failing to plan is planning to fail' becomes most relevant at a time when something has gone wrong. This is one of the main reasons why thorough planning at an operational level is more likely to lead to positive sales results. Planning impacts on the way your company is run which affects its sales revenue, profits and the business relationships with customers and suppliers.

This chapter looks at:

- **Evaluating performance.**
- **Short, medium and long-term planning.**
- **Preparing for change.**

As highlighted in Chapter 2, *Creating a sales and marketing strategy*, many companies have an informal business plan and sales strategy, which is not always clearly defined. By being proactive and taking more managerial responsibility for this, you improve your chances of retaining customers and achieving sales growth. This chapter will help you to implement your sales strategy by developing relevant action plans.

Evaluating performance

The previous two chapters looked at understanding your market and developing a sales and marketing strategy. The learning points from this need to be implemented so that when you evaluate your sales performance from a planning perspective, you have taken these areas into account.

This chapter looks at how you can implement action plans which will support the goals you are looking to achieve. As part of developing a sales operations plan you should introduce a formal process to measure your sales performance. There might be a number of 'triggers' for this, for example:

- The end of a financial year.
- A time when you might be looking to expand.
- Economic uncertainty.
- As part of a regular business review.

Whenever you complete this process you should look at evaluating how well your company is performing relative to its goals. This does not only relate to a financial audit but should include other elements such as selling skills and processes. Some business owners don't always take the time to do this or may not be convinced of the benefit.

By formally evaluating your sales performance at regular intervals you are in a better position to assess the existing position of your company and its potential to grow.

The sales performance evaluation process

A process to evaluate performance can be useful for a number of reasons, including reducing uncertainty and giving an objective view of how you are performing in a number of key business areas. It is good management practice and can help to avoid costly mistakes. One simple method of evaluation derives from research on management training development by Easterby-Smith (1998). For example, if you are trying to:

1. Show that a particular course of action has worked – to **Prove** that it works.
2. Ensure that a course of action was implemented properly – to check that the **Control** mechanisms work.
3. Ensure that sales objectives have been effective – so that your objectives do actually **Improve** the results.
4. Ensure that the sales operation is progressing, both individually and as a group – **Learn** from experience.

What to evaluate will depend on your sales goals for this process. Evaluation might include looking at:

- Sales performance appraisals, including training, coaching and development.
- A particular part of your company which you think could be improved.
- The effect of government legislation on your pricing structure (e.g. the impact of a change in relation to business related taxation).
- The success of new products or services you have introduced.

Prioritising is a vital step of this process.

PRACTICAL EXAMPLE

A company identified that in order to get better value for money and become more effective it would recruit double the number of graduates (rather than experienced sales executives) for its sales operation. While this saved money, it didn't take into account their lack of experience or the time it would take to train them with effective selling skills as part of the new recruitment process.

This meant that the goals were not achieved and the management had to go back to their original policy of hiring more experienced sales executives, and invest more as a consequence.

When understanding the needs of your sales operation, make sure that you consider all stakeholders. This can help the process to remain more objective. Few business owners would purport to be experts in all areas of sales, marketing, finance, etc.

Some aspects of evaluation are subjective and it isn't always easy to measure performance (i.e. in a non-sales role) or how well a combination of departments or individuals might be working together. This is why it is important to be clear about the aims of an evaluation and the ways to achieve it.

A model taken from the *Double-Loop Learning* technique offers a good example of how this process can be developed. This was devised by Argyris and Schon (1978) and looks at:

1. Underlying *assumptions* of a particular plan or strategy.
2. The *goals* which are set from it.
3. The *results* (and consequences of the actions that are carried out).

This means that if the outcomes of a particular goal are not met, the easiest option for a business owner might be to simply set another goal. This is an example of *Single-Loop Learning*.

However, a more productive solution is to look at the assumptions which underpin the goal-setting to see if any of them need to be changed (which is *Double-Loop Learning*). This means that the original strategy can be adapted, rather than new goals being continually set if they aren't working. This can be illustrated in the following way using a typical sales goal:

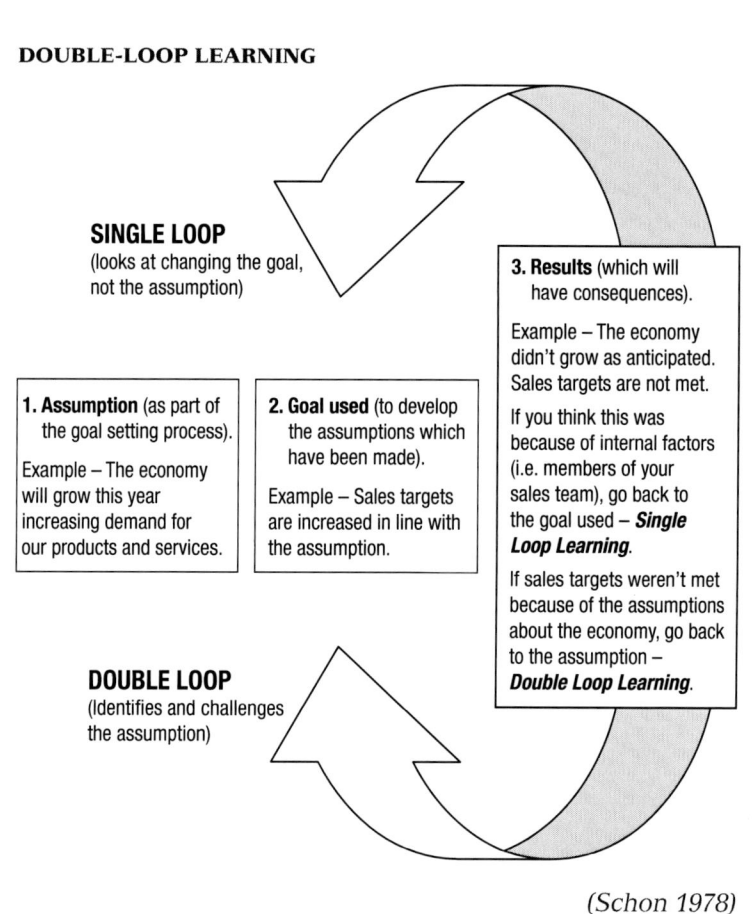

DOUBLE-LOOP LEARNING

SINGLE LOOP
(looks at changing the goal, not the assumption)

1. Assumption (as part of the goal setting process).

Example – The economy will grow this year increasing demand for our products and services.

2. Goal used (to develop the assumptions which have been made).

Example – Sales targets are increased in line with the assumption.

3. Results (which will have consequences).

Example – The economy didn't grow as anticipated. Sales targets are not met.

If you think this was because of internal factors (i.e. members of your sales team), go back to the goal used – *Single Loop Learning*.

If sales targets weren't met because of the assumptions about the economy, go back to the assumption – *Double Loop Learning*.

DOUBLE LOOP
(Identifies and challenges the assumption)

(Schon 1978)

As this example indicates, reducing the sales targets may or may not be the best option. By looking at the assumptions which underpin the goals, a true understanding of what is needed is much easier to achieve.

The reason why *Double-Loop Learning* is such a good way to develop a particular strategy in relation to sales is that it will help a business owner to experiment. It will also help identify and then challenge any underlying assumptions which are made in relation to setting goals as part of the sales planning process.

In order for this to work you will need to be flexible and patient if a particular strategy doesn't work immediately. The *Double-Loop Learning* model can also be put in a table for you to assess how to manage these steps. To achieve this, consider something in your company which needs to be evaluated internally and use the following table to think about the relevant outcome:

EXERCISE

Steps	Outcome
As part of the planning process complete steps 1 – 5	
1. List your top sales goals.	
2. On a scale of 1-10, how achievable are the goals?	
3. List what processes you have to monitor the goals.	
4. What measurement will you use to assess the goals?	
5. List the assumptions which you have formulated as part of your goal setting.	

By using this evaluation method you allow yourself to adopt a realistic and open approach. You can then make modifications. However, although you can factor in a degree of error, uncertainty is still part of everyday sales planning. But this process will give you the benefit of having different perspectives as to how and why something did or didn't happen the way you anticipated.

Remember, it is easier to be flexible if your goals are realistic. Effective evaluation processes will lead to performance improvement.

Performance improvement

Many companies often find that they don't have the time, application or perceived need for constant re-evaluation. It can be challenging if you are pushed in many directions as a business owner. This might include being under staffed, as well as trying to meet your sales revenue targets.

Having well-trained employees that are motivated will help you to retain them as well as improve your sales performance and maintain customer loyalty. However, much depends on how you spend your time and resources. For example, some companies might see ongoing development as a good investment; others might focus on developing better sales processes.

It is good practice to look regularly at how to continue improving all aspects of your business, not only as part of the drive for more sales! *The European Foundation for Quality Management (EFQM, 2000)* outlined a business *Model of Excellence* which is widely used to help achieve this aim. It can be adapted to look at different aspects of sales performance, five points of which focus on 'what to do' regarding good business practice. This adapted version includes:

1. Being an effective leader.
2. Having strong management skills.
3. Having a clear business strategy.
4. Developing good business relationships (with target accounts and customers).
5. Using reliable internal business processes.

Think about how well you do in these key areas. You can form an *Action Plan* in order to help you with this and can create your own *Model of Excellence*. This involves looking at the above five points and:

- Describing a relevant business situation that relates to each category.
- Giving yourself a Good, Average or Poor rating of how you think you did in each category.
- Listing how you could improve in each area.

The table gives a typical example and then allows you to add your own scenarios.

EXERCISE
CREATING YOUR OWN BUSINESS MODEL

Business topic	Current situation Describe an internal situation in the areas below.	Your rating Give yourself a rating, i.e. Good, Average, Poor).	Actions What plans can you make to improve your current situation?
Leadership (people focused)			
Example	You might feel that there are times when you could be more positive and praise people more.	Average	Take time to praise someone who does something well and exceeds your expectations.
Your example			
Management skills (task focused)			
Example	You might postpone meetings by taking on too many commitments.	Average	Delegate more and manage your diary and time better.
Your example			

Business and sales strategy (ongoing and formal reviews)

Example	You might not make enough time for future business planning.	**Poor**	Set up a board meeting with directors to develop this and agree timeframes for actions.
Your example			

Business relationships (with colleagues and customers)

Example	You do allow time to meet with your largest customers.	**Good**	Continue with this and look at how to continue to grow the business relationships.

Internal processes (e.g. order or sales processing)

Example	You need to improve some areas of your sales order processing.	**Average**	Talk with your IT provider to look at updating the current sales order system.
Your example			

This type of action plan, adapted from the *EFQM model*, will help you develop a broader view of your sales performance. You may find that there are times when you can't implement every idea at once. However, you should take time to develop your leadership and management skills.

Your internal operations and customers should be at the forefront of your thinking here. This is because if you improve areas internally, you will then increase your chances of reacting to changes in the market. This will also make it easier to develop your sales and marketing strategy. The investment of time in this will help you to have a better perspective of where you planned to be and where you should be in the future.

This section has looked at the value of assessing your current business performance. This reinforces the need to have plans in place to list and measure the steps you need to take to improve. This requires choosing the right actions, prioritising them and, most importantly, following through on their implementation.

Short, medium and long-term planning

Formalising a sales plan

The next step in implementing your strategy is to think about realistic timeframes for the plans you want to develop. This will involve a short, medium and long-term focus. You will need to define these three areas and for clarity, the stages can be described in the following way:

- Short-term: 1 – 12 months.
- Medium-term: 1 – 3 years.
- Long-term: 3 years (and beyond).

This involves breaking a plan down into manageable parts in relation to the size of tasks, their priority and the actual time each one will take. In line with your sales and marketing strategy, involve key members of your management and sales team in the planning process.

There are some best-practice suggestions which you will want to progress, for example:

- Ensure that you create the right internal structure to make your plans successful. Ask yourself about whether you have the right people and how they might need to adapt to any proposed changes to ensure your objectives have the best chance of working.

- Be aware of how effective your internal sales processes are. For example, ensure that you have a system which allows clear internal communication.

- Ensure that key individuals are aware of the responsibility they have and that they also have the authority to carry out any changes to your plan. People sometimes believe that they have the responsibility but not necessarily the authority to implement a sales-related task. This can limit them in carrying the task out effectively.

- Think about what can and can't be achieved. There is nothing worse than embarking on a plan and failing only because it was too ambitious. Also ensure that you have a realistic timeframe in place.

- Break down any barriers or resistance to change by selling the benefits of a plan to the relevant staff. Have empathy with individuals – many people don't like change. Some resist it because they fear the change will make them worse off (or they will have to work harder). This is why having an assertive and patient approach to sales planning is essential.

Now, you need to go into more detail to create a sales operations plan, for example:

- How to implement the plan.
- How to manage the sales team responsible for the plan.
- Having a list of actions (and a timeframe to work towards).
- Monitoring the plan to make sure it is working as you want it to.

The following table can be created to illustrate this. It gives a typical example and then allows you to add your own scenarios.

SALES OPERATIONS PLAN

Steps	Your Plan
Implement the plan (with realistic timeframes)	
Example	You might have set new sales targets and want to review them every quarter of the current year.
Your example	
Manage the sales team (list actions)	
Example	You realise that to achieve this goal you will need to have more regular sales meetings.
Your example	
Put your plan into action (list actions and timeframes)	
Example	You set dates for the sales meetings with specific agendas, action points and timeframes.
Your example	
Monitor (list what actually happens and correct if necessary)	
Example	You find that the more regular sales meetings have been well received. One change that has come out of them is the need to improve the way that sales opportunities are developed.
Your example	

If a plan isn't monitored then it is difficult to measure the outcome effectively. By doing this well it is easier to make any necessary changes. This type of flexibility will give everyone confidence and make the plan more likely to succeed. Having a process to manage the plan is also important.

Sales action plans

A *Sales Action Plan* is a part of the planning process that focuses on what is actually being done, along with agreed timeframes. It helps break down the operational plan into individual tasks and assigns the responsibility of delivering them. This might seem obvious, but not every company communicates how it could be delivered in a manageable way. It can also apply to a particular project you might have.

A plan can also emanate from a review of your sales and marketing strategy. This could relate to a product or service you sell, perhaps one which is under-performing. This might involve something that you feel the need to change. But it needs to be progressed in a logical way, by looking at:

- A start and end date.
- Which people should be involved.
- How you will implement it.
- What resources you need.
- The business benefits.

This can be listed in a simple table to focus you on the task, and then shared with your sales and management team. The following table continues on from the earlier examples in relation to an operational plan, and then allows you to give your own.

EXERCISE
SALES ACTION PLAN

Steps to be taken	Start date	End date	People involved	Implementation process and resources needed	Business benefits
Improve sales forecasting	Month 1	Month 3	Business owner, sales manager and one sales executive.	Discussions with the sales team about improving monthly sales forecasts. Agree revised plan, then involve team members – and communicate it.	Convert more opportunities to sales
Your examples					

You can create your own *Sales Action Plan* more graphically by producing a Gantt chart (a bar chart showing a schedule). It can help you to implement sales tasks efficiently and allows you to manage the allocation of resources to complete the sales planning process.

In order to create your action plan, follow these steps:

1. Make a decision on what tasks are needed to be completed.

2. Calculate how long the individual tasks will take.

3. Commit the amount of time needed for each task.

4. Create a schedule with this information.
5. Delegate the tasks to a sales manager (or a member of the sales team).
6. Build in an additional 10 per cent 'safety net' timeframe.

The following example replicates the one in the sales action plan and lists the actions needed to improve the sales forecasting process. This includes particular tasks and a likely timeframe for completion. You can adapt this to make it relevant to you by choosing your own criteria.

GANTT CHART EXAMPLE
(in relation to improving the sales forecasting process)

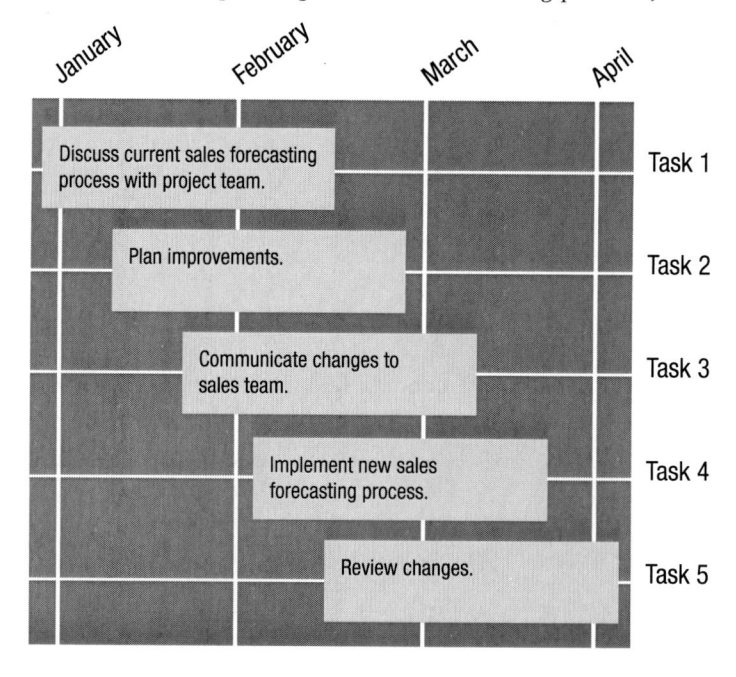

	January	February	March	April	
Discuss current sales forecasting process with project team.					Task 1
	Plan improvements.				Task 2
		Communicate changes to sales team.			Task 3
		Implement new sales forecasting process.			Task 4
			Review changes.		Task 5

Additional data that could be considered for a Gantt chart includes:

- Details of particular tasks you want to put in the action plan.
- What actions might be dependent upon others (e.g. opening a new office could be dependent upon recruiting sales executives by a certain date).
- The level of resources you have available.
- The importance of a particular action that could affect the timeframe.
- Monitoring then reviewing all of the above.

You can colour code different categories to highlight and differentiate them for presentation purposes.

Effective sales planning involves preparation, being adaptable, sound implementation and a degree of measurement. The time you invest in this will help you implement your sales strategy. It will also help with another vital element in the planning process – managing change.

Preparing for change

In order to make profits and achieve sales growth your customers need to be consistently satisfied in relation to the products, service, business relationship and value that you offer. This can be influenced by the way your company is structured.

Groups that can affect your business relationships internally and externally include:

Internal

- Shareholders.

- Your management team.
- Other employees.
- Your own family (some of whom might own part of/work in the business).

External
- Customers.
- Lenders (e.g. banks).
- Suppliers of products and services to you.
- Local and central government.

This can be expressed in the following way:

GROUPS THAT CAN BE AFFECTED BY YOUR COMPANY

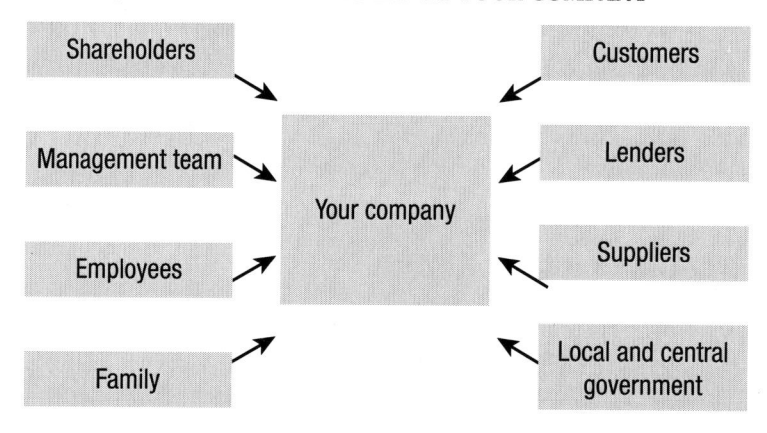

```
Shareholders  ↘                    ↙  Customers
Management team  ↘                 ↙  Lenders
                   Your company
Employees  ↗                       ↖  Suppliers
Family  ↗                          ↖  Local and central government
```

It is worth spending time reviewing your own (internal and external) stakeholders, their priorities and the time invested in looking after them. Even if you have a strong focus on customer retention, conflicts of interest can still occur. Business owners often have to look at a trade-off between conflicting objectives and what can and can't be planned for. This includes:

- Short versus medium-term profit returns to shareholders.
- Individual employee motivation and internal agendas.
- Family changes, concerns or priorities.
- Changing lender criteria/economic conditions.
- Government legislation.

This is why consideration needs to be given to these issues in terms of the time they take up and their level of importance. This will involve being adaptable and having the ability to accept changes in the way your company is run.

Change is something that every business owner should accept. The speed of change in an economically challenging and technology-driven world is fast. Companies have to be dynamic, pro-active and be able to calculate risk. Failure to adapt to a changing business environment can lead to a loss of customers and reduced profits. This can put your company under financial pressure.

If you embrace change and prepare for it, you will be in a better position to grow. The market you are in often forces change upon you, which is why a degree of flexibility will be needed. This can be illustrated in the table below, which looks at the types of change that can happen, along with internal and external examples.

INTERNAL AND EXTERNAL CHANGE

Type of change	Internal example	External example
Company re-evaluation	Desire to change next year's targets due to increased sales growth.	Economy forces a decision to stay in the existing building for a further two years rather than moving to larger premises.
Technology	Decision to invest in new computer system.	Realisation that your products or services need to be sold on the Internet.
Finance	Need for new investment.	Increase in business taxes.
People	Company restructure.	Sales recruitment drive and external help with this.
Customer led	Customer's expectations rise and product/services need improving.	Need for your supplier to improve product design or manufacture.

The challenges listed here should encourage you to think about change and the importance it will have on sales planning in the months and years ahead.

You might want to gauge how pro-active and ready for change you are! In order to assess this, answer 'yes', 'no' or 'not sure' to the following questions.

EXERCISE

	Change questions	Your answer (yes, no or not sure)	Describe the change and the course of action?
1.	Have any changes that you have made in the past year been out of your control?		
2.	Have you made any changes in the past year but found them difficult to implement?		
3.	Do your employees react well to change?		
4.	Do you tend to make quick decisions regarding changing something internally?		
5.	If you have introduced any change process, have you monitored the outcome?		

Think about the consequences of your answers and what course of action might need to be taken. Also, think about what impact it might be having on your sales team, other related departments and day-to-day business issues. Like other parts of the sales operational planning process, any change needs to:

- Be well planned and communicated.
- Include timeframes.
- Involve relevant directors, managers (and other members of staff).
- Have a clearly defined and communicated benefit.

By taking the time to do this you will increase the chances of any change process working. A survey in relation to change by Buchanan, Claydon and Doyle (1999) had some interesting outcomes. Of those who either agreed or strongly agreed with a change:

- 96% of managers saw 'change management as central to the performance of their organisation'.
- 96% also thought that there was 'a need to manage continuing change, not just discrete change projects'.
- 67% thought that most people took change for granted.
- 63% thought that they knew what changes to introduce but admitted having problems with an effective implementation strategy.

However, only 39% could agree that a change had been successful.

This shows that as a business owner, being ready to make changes will help you adapt to the future.

Adapting to change involves flexibility and good communication. It will mean delegating some tasks in order to share the responsibility needed to make any change successful and to make it become part of every employee's daily routine.

Chapter summary

This chapter covered three main areas:

- Evaluating performance.
- Short, medium and long-term planning.
- Preparing for change.

Having a sales operations plan will make it easier for a business owner to make objective decisions. It will help to increase sales performance by becoming part of your short, medium and long-term planning. You need to take the time to think about planning.

Any changes you implement in order to facilitate this process should be factored into your plans. You will need to communicate the benefits of change in order for them to be accepted. These types of initiatives can also have a positive effect on retaining customers.

Key points

✓ Develop a sales operations planning process and monitor it.

✓ Think about how your planning process links to your sales and marketing strategy.

✓ Break your plans into short, medium and long-term stages.

✓ Think about customer retention and the changes you need to make to achieve sales growth.

Chapter 4
Getting the best out of a sales CRM system

Chapter 4
Getting the best out of a sales CRM system

This chapter looks at making the most out of the information used by your sales operation. This will lead business owners to make better decisions by focusing on the right areas and having objective and subjective information to support this.

The two key areas that will be looked at are:

- **Managing sales information effectively.**

- **Combining data and knowledge to create value.**

In order to capture and store the right sales data and information you will need to consider the type of IT systems you use to support your sales operation. Installing an effective *Customer Relationship Management (CRM) system* can help to increase customer retention. This can be done by tracking sales opportunities and managing the information required to build business relationships.

Managing sales information effectively

One of the challenges any business owner faces is the storage, retrieval and use of sales data; for example, pricing, credit days, marketing information and delivery schedules. This also needs to include database, contact and sales pipeline management, etc.

Many SMEs develop their internal sales and support systems in an ill defined way. This can mean that electronic communication between departments often relies on more than one system. This can cause issues with the reporting of information, which can prove ineffective and time consuming.

That is why it is a good idea to think about how you can access different types of sales information easily. By doing this you not only increase your chances of improving the quality of your information but also your internal and external business communication. An effective CRM system can help you achieve this. If you use a system well, it will also help you to reduce your costs by being more efficient and thereby saving time. This will increase your value to customers.

CRM systems can be server or web-based. They can be bought in a standard format, in which case there is usually some degree of flexibility in adapting them for your use, or they can be bought from specialist resellers suited to a particular type of market. The latter allows you to tailor the system to manage your own particular sales and business data.

There can be issues of confidentiality as well as internal and external communication. With the advent of CRM systems, storing data and improving communication has been made much easier, but it does rely on a number of factors, including:

- The quality of the data you input.

- Sales information being kept up-to-date.
- Relevant reports being created (for sales management purposes).
- Minimum standards of use.
- Creating different levels of user rights.

Any CRM system is only as good as the data and information it stores. Systems are likely to have calendar, diary and email facilities. You should also have the ability to attach files to a customer (or target account) record, as well as alerts if agreed actions are not completed on time. The most important thing is to ensure that it is practical and relevant for your company.

It enables users to note the outcomes of telephone calls and customer meetings. In terms of functionality, there is often a link between *Front Office* (sales and marketing information) and *Back Office* (finance, operations and production data). This is an important feature otherwise you might have to use two different systems which may not have the potential to be integrated.

An example of how a CRM system is designed to work can be illustrated in the following way:

EXAMPLE OF A CRM SYSTEM

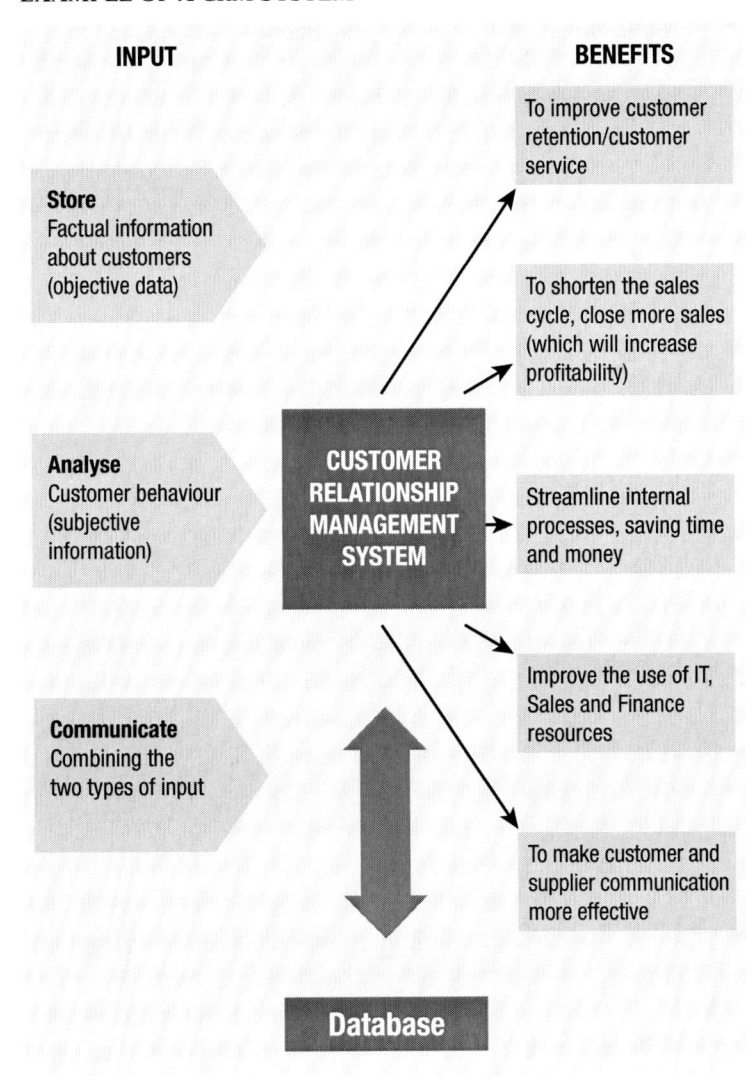

INPUT

Store
Factual information about customers (objective data)

Analyse
Customer behaviour (subjective information)

Communicate
Combining the two types of input

→ **CUSTOMER RELATIONSHIP MANAGEMENT SYSTEM** ↕ **Database**

BENEFITS

- To improve customer retention/customer service
- To shorten the sales cycle, close more sales (which will increase profitability)
- Streamline internal processes, saving time and money
- Improve the use of IT, Sales and Finance resources
- To make customer and supplier communication more effective

This illustration breaks down the type of data input, i.e. the ability to store, analyse and communicate information. This comes with significant benefits, if the system is used effectively, i.e. the streamlining of different sales-related processes.

PRACTICAL POINTER

Any CRM system is only as good as the data and information it contains, and how well and how often people use it.

Advantages of CRM systems

It is a good exercise to re-look at the functionality of your own CRM system if you have one or to look at the benefits of investing in one if you don't. It will give you the ability to:

- See the 'bigger picture', i.e. to study a certain part of a customer's business or a particular part of where an opportunity lies in your sales pipeline.

- Identify relevant data quickly and easily. This can then be communicated and shared internally or with a target account or customer.

If used correctly any CRM system should help you and, in particular, your sales team to input, co-ordinate and retrieve information essential to their daily role. This next example relates to a company and contact information summary within a sales forecasting software programme. It can be used as part of a tailored CRM system.

SALES FORECASTING EXAMPLE

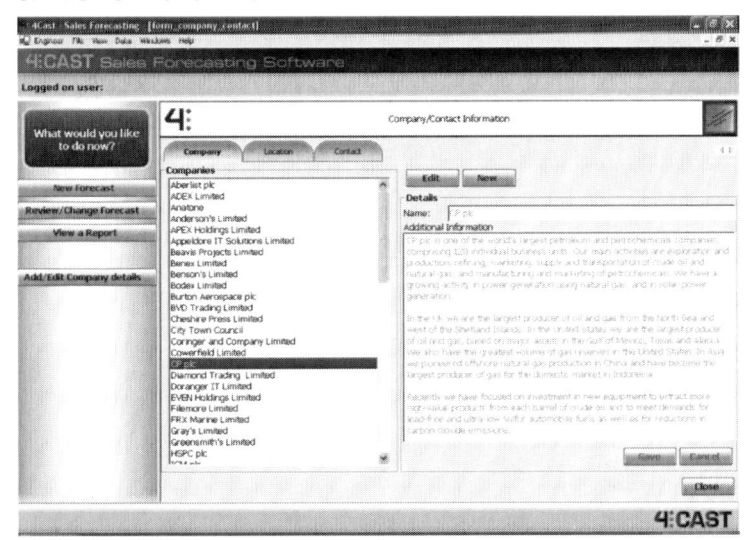

Reports in CRM systems can summarise data or events to help you manage sales information.

So far we have looked at the benefits of CRM systems, but if they are not used properly or for the right reasons, these benefits will diminish!

Why CRM systems can fail to deliver their potential

Many companies fail to manage sales information effectively or to set minimum standards of use or reporting. It is essential to monitor CRM system usage in seeking to provide effective internal and external communication.

Other reasons for a reduced level of effectiveness can include:

- A poor planning and implementation process, often caused by a lack of understanding of what it actually is that you want from the system.

- Over-focusing on the sales aspect of the system without considering how it integrates with other 'back office' functions like finance and distribution.
- Not giving enough respect to the service element of the system, i.e. looking at things from a customer perspective *after* a sale takes place.
- Not rolling out the system in a staged manner.
- Not selling the benefits of the system to the users or not having good internal communication.
- Expecting the system to increase your sales and effectiveness but without the necessary investment of time and resource to manage this.

These points are important if you want to get the most out of any CRM system.

Retaining the right type of sales information

Opinions on buyers and target accounts generally have to be carefully stored in a CRM system due to Data Protection. This can give a company or an individual the right to know what information you have stored about them.

In some ways a CRM system replicates how parts of our own memory work. Few people can retain information in their memories in relation to sales for a long period of time. Any information from customer meetings is often transferred to a digital format as a method of retaining facts and opinions.

Subjectivity is interesting because our memories change over time. This can lead to the distortion of a situation; so, encourage users to be objective!

It is important for any user of a system to take the time to input relevant information. If this isn't done there can be a tendency for sales executives and managers to:

- Use their own methods separately.
- Rely on their own memory rather than input any data.
- Rely on the CRM system to do their selling for them!

This can devalue a sales role and bring about a more 'commodity' selling style. To avoid this, ensure that you introduce some rules about how your system is going to work. While you don't want the CRM system to control how someone sells, it needs to be used in the right way.

This will help you to manage information effectively, although you will still need to identify the type of information to input. You will also need to decide how it links to your values as well as your sales and marketing strategy.

Combining data and knowledge to create value

A CRM system needs to be a support mechanism for a sales operation. It can be an excellent way to provide factual or statistical data but cannot guarantee *how* information is interpreted.

Managing a sales team requires more than having a good CRM system or sales process. Users need to understand the benefits of inputting information and keeping it up-to-date. If you don't take the time to do this you could find that the sales team:

- Spend too much time inputting the information.

- Don't understand how to use the information to develop business relationships.
- Can't see the relevance of guidelines.
- Don't buy in to what you are trying to achieve.
- See a CRM system primarily as a management tool to control them.

You may want to promote an internal discussion with other directors to establish what information and specific actions are needed to get the best use out of your CRM system.

A typical system allows you to import database information and contains *objective* data (e.g. contracts and target account information) as well as *subjective* information (e.g. customer behaviour and actions related to developing a sale and the business relationship).

The building and management of a CRM system will involve input from your IT Department and your computer systems provider. Good communication between a sales team and management team is important to ensure that a system works well.

In order to communicate information effectively it is useful to review the process of communication within your sales team. This can be examined using an adapted version of Shannon's *Communication Model* (1948). It covers four areas:

1. **An information source** – The data held on the system.
2. **Transmission** – A method to transmit the data, (i.e. the type of system used).
3. **Reception** – The sales individual who is receiving the information.
4. **Interpretation** – How the information is interpreted.

Shannon explained how effective communication can lead to good performance. The model is also a useful tool when you are looking to maximise internal and external communication. This can be illustrated in the following way:

COMMUNICATION MODEL

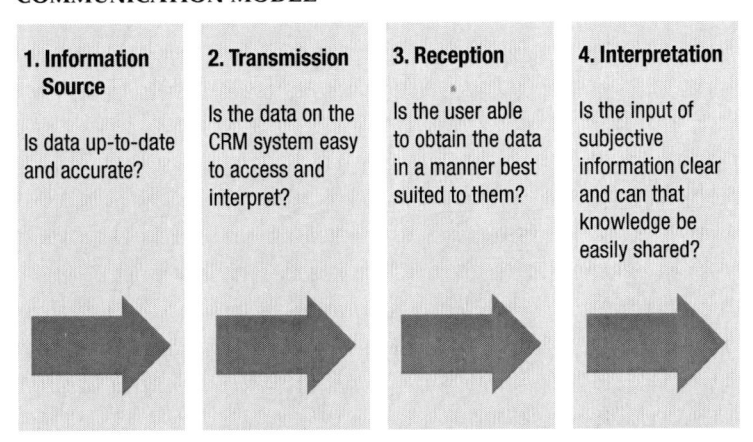

1. Information Source	2. Transmission	3. Reception	4. Interpretation
Is data up-to-date and accurate?	Is the data on the CRM system easy to access and interpret?	Is the user able to obtain the data in a manner best suited to them?	Is the input of subjective information clear and can that knowledge be easily shared?

(Shannon 1948)

While capturing relevant data is vital, there can be the tendency to put in information which is not always useful! This is why you should make it clear how you plan to use sales data and information.

You should also maximise the use of your CRM system by being aware of any gaps in relation to information you have and what you still need.

Distinguishing between 'known and unknown' sales information

Many companies develop a culture in which sales information is known but isn't recognised as something that requires formal capture. When you are doing well, this might not seem so relevant. But when you are under pressure, the quality of data can help to produce effective sales and marketing campaigns.

There are dangers in not taking the time to ensure that users 'buy in' to using your CRM system properly. This is particularly relevant if:

- Sales performance needs to be improved quickly.
- If a sales executive leaves.
- Changes in the market put sudden demands on the company.

In this context, these examples can have a negative impact on a sales operation and can affect its sales performance. You should therefore be aware of what your sales operation needs to know compared with what it does know in relation to your target market. That is why it is important to be clear about the type of knowledge you are looking to capture.

Jordan and Jones (1997) compared information that is already known and areas that need to be identified. For example:

What we know….	What we don't know….
1. What our marketing budget is.	1. What is the best way to ensure the marketing budget is spent effectively.
2. What revenue needs to be generated in order to meet sales targets.	2. Ways in which we might increase revenue by 'working smarter'.
3. Which target market we want to focus on in the future.	3. The best ways to apply our existing skill set and develop in new markets.

Once this exercise has been completed the next step is to decide what information can be retained and what needs to be managed differently.

Some information is not always easy to record in a uniform way as it relies on a degree of subjectivity. This means that the development of a successful CRM system needs to take into account how well users are trained. It also needs to be shared, to ensure that relevant people are aware of the type of sales information you want to capture.

To achieve this, you should ensure that you are aware of what knowledge and experience exists in your sales operation. You then need to develop a CRM system that reflects this, so that shared information can help improve your communication. This can be illustrated in the following way:

IMPROVING SKILLS BASED KNOWLEDGE

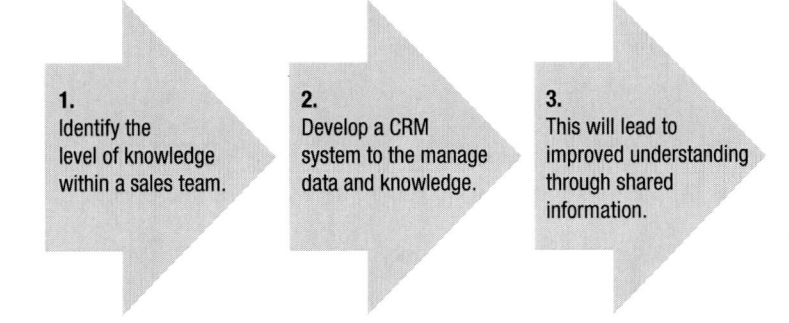

1. Identify the level of knowledge within a sales team.

2. Develop a CRM system to the manage data and knowledge.

3. This will lead to improved understanding through shared information.

The integration of your company's skills, processes, learning and knowledge are key factors that will affect the successful implementation of your sales strategy.

One final thought about combining process and knowledge is to ensure that any CRM system isn't used in a punitive way.

This will help you get the best out of your sales team in order to create value.

Getting extra value out of your CRM system

You will need to create some rules which apply to getting the most out of any data storage system. This is why it is a good idea to have minimum standards to help you decide what type of information you need to capture.

By having a set of rules in place you increase your chances of positive communication. This will lead to your sales team having a better understanding of what is going well and, if there are sales issues, resolving them early in the process. This will help to improve customer relations and maximise customer retention.

When sales revenues and profits are high it can be easy to ignore the discipline that a strong sales process can demand. But, in uncertain economic conditions attention to detail can expose some members of a sales team! This is because people might not input essential information into the CRM system. For example:

- Update target account/existing customer contacts.
- Meeting dates, agendas, outcomes and next steps.
- Accurate sales pipeline information.
- Potential sales 'blocks' which might stop a sale progressing.
- Lack of up-to-date sales or financial data.

You can only get the best out of the system if people are trained to use it properly and it is used regularly. By doing this, you make the selling process much easier and create an edge over your competitors.

This is the point where – **'Process + Knowledge = VALUE'**

Creating this type of value will help you develop *USPs*. Other elements to consider include ensuring that you don't have one rule for one user and one for another (with the same level of user rights). If a sales executive is doing well it shouldn't mean that they don't have to use the system correctly, but someone under target does! This will send out the wrong message and will limit your chances of getting the long-term type of sales behaviour you are looking for.

Another key point is that if successful sales executives leave, it is important that you have captured the relevant sales information. This should include their views on how target accounts and customers are being developed.

Sales information can be devalued if someone leaves and looks to pass this to a competitor (who might be that person's next employer)! There are laws to protect companies against sales executives doing this, but you should also decide which target accounts need senior management input in order to build multiple-level relationships.

In order to manage a sales *issue*, think about its *effect* and a possible *solution*. This can be illustrated in the following table, which gives examples and then allows you to create your own.

ISSUE, EFFECT AND SOLUTION

	Issue	Effect	Solution
1.	A sales executive decides to leave.	Information is missing or knowledge gaps appear in the CRM system or in a customer relationship.	• Carry out an account review before the person leaves and visit important customers. • Ensure that CRM knowledge is intact. • Ensure a new sales executive follows and maintains agreed sales process standards.
	Your example		
2.	Maintaining a CRM system takes time.	Not everyone uses it in the right way by not updating the system.	• Get some agreed minimum standards in place. • Encourage regular use of the system to help users focus. • Reinforce the benefits.
	Your example		
3.	Sales Executives don't use the system properly as it is seen as complicated.	Resentment from other users causing the system not to be fully maximised.	• Devise a system which is easy to operate and get 'buy in' from the users. • Get all relevant levels of management to understand the system. • Set agreed targets for this. • Ensure every user is trained.
	Your example		

	Issue	Effect	Solution
4.	Information is out of date.	Loss of credibility or business with customers.	• Ensure regular updates are done. • IT department/contact should set reminders in key areas to help. • Set out benefits of keeping the system up-to-date.
	Your example		
5.	Management don't have time to monitor its use.	Sets a bad example and allows misuse.	• Set a good example by using it and have agreed user rights. • Ensure the system is designed to benefit everyone, including managers. • Get help from your IT department/contact with management reports and updates.
	Your example		

Now look at your top five issues, their effect and what solutions you can put in place.

You will also need to consider the impact of introducing a CRM system on a sales and support team and how it can have a positive impact on sales performance. Getting the best out of your sales team in relation to recording, sharing and developing information does take time to set up and review.

By doing this and encouraging people, you will be in a better position to implement your sales strategy by managing the entire sales process. This will lead to increased customer retention, reduced costs and improved communication. It will also add more value to relationships with customers and target accounts, making you an easier company to do business with.

Chapter summary

This chapter covered two main areas:

- Managing sales information effectively.
- Combining data and knowledge to create value.

Installing a CRM system is a good way to store and manage information, provided it is used effectively. This information can then be used to develop an account as well as for good internal communication and planning.

To create real value you will need to get the 'buy in' from users as well as set minimum standards and user rights. There also needs to be a strong focus on the type of sales information you put into the system. The quality of the knowledge that exists within the sales team and how this is transferred to your CRM system will also be a determining factor of its success.

Key points

- ✓ When installing a CRM system, think about what type of data and information you store and how it will be used.
- ✓ Monitor what works well and what doesn't in your own system.
- ✓ Focus on the quality of the information input by your sales team in order to create value.
- ✓ Make the process for capturing, storing and communicating information easy to achieve.

**Chapter 5
How to improve your
decision-making**

Chapter 5
How to improve your decision-making

When implementing your sales strategy, making the right decisions will have a significant impact on the ability to generate revenue. This chapter looks at how business owners can improve their decision-making by having a better understanding of the people who work in their sales operation. It includes:

- **Understanding behaviour.**
- **How your management style can improve sales performance.**

To manage a sales operation well, it is necessary to look at the reasons why people behave like they do. This type of understanding will help you to get the best out of them in terms of focus and sales performance.

The chapter looks at the importance of understanding the perceptions of business owners and people in a sales operation. Trying to understand someone's point of view will help you to remain objective in order to make the right decisions for your company.

Understanding behaviour

One of the most common challenges business owners face, is to know their own character well and the people in their sales operation. This is important because it will help you in the decision-making process, allowing you to adapt to different people in different situations. Knowing yourself is the first step in the process of managing other people well.

Getting a group of people in a sales environment to work together often begins with knowing what motivates them. Most team behaviour relates to helping someone in the hope that you might want that person's help in the future. However, in a sales environment, where targets are involved, there will also be an element of competition and single-mindedness. Many sales executives will think at one time or another, 'what's in it for me?' This can lead to a conflict between:

- What someone else wants.
- What you want.
- What is good for the company.

If you are the business owner it is easier to do what you want, but if this is at the expense of others, it can lead to resentment and a lack of enthusiasm from the people you manage, especially in sales. A forceful management style can also lack objectivity, i.e. if you impose decisions rather than look for compromise (see Chapter 6, *A strategy to manage different types of people*).

In order to look at how objective you are about your character and that of others, make a list of the personality traits that you like about yourself, so that you can develop them.

EXERCISE

Traits I like:
-
-
-

Traits I need to work on:
-
-
-

Look at how these traits impact on your sales operation. Consider the consequences that result from this and ones which might affect your sales performance. Think also about how others interact with you in different situations.

Be aware of your own personality traits. This doesn't need to be formalised, but by thinking about your own behaviour, you improve the chances of good communication and understanding other people's perspectives.

If someone is naturally predisposed to a certain type of behaviour this doesn't mean that it has to be accepted or can't be changed (including yours)! The impact of change is something that you will relate to as your company grows.

A group of people working for you will often need to adapt to new initiatives. This is why you have to be adaptable too. However, there can be potential conflict between how individuals want to behave and how you want them to behave in order to achieve the sales and business goals.

One of the common challenges when employing someone in a sales role is the expectation that the successful applicant can deliver the results that you need. The interview process is replaced by the reality of how that person performs on a daily basis. In the future, if sales executives don't hit their targets or meet *Key Performance Indicators (KPIs)*, your relationship with them is likely to change.

You will have to decide what you can and can't influence with members of your sales team in relation to their characters and level of sales experience. Also, consider the context of the situation with regard to the economic climate and how your company is performing in its market (which was discussed in Chapter 1, *Responding to changes in the market*).

Understanding a person's attitude

A key factor in determining people's behaviour at work in your sales operation (and the workplace generally) is their attitude! Where does this emanate from?

There is a correlation between someone's personality traits (which involve genetic factors) and that person's upbringing (experiences and environment). While you cannot be expected to know everything about someone's past experiences and beliefs, it is worth noting their attitude in relation to work and what makes them think in a particular way. This will give you a better chance of influencing someone.

Over time, you will develop an understanding of people's attitudes in relation to their social and work situation. You will no doubt compare their background and experience with your own. This will help you understand their perspective on situations and why it may differ from yours.

In order to get the type of behaviour you want, you need to think about the way you communicate with others. You will need to look at how someone reacts to being asked to do different tasks. This is particularly relevant in getting a sales team to understand the need of meeting the targets you set. By doing this you increase the chances of a response being positive and requests being carried out more effectively.

Spooncer (1992) looked at how different types of behaviour can result from a person's attitude. He defined a strong relationship between how someone feels about something (based on their emotions) and how this fits in with their current beliefs (based on their previous experience). He predicted that this will determine the type of behaviour (and following actions) that can be expected from someone. This can be illustrated in the following way:

HOW ATTITUDE CAN AFFECT BEHAVIOUR

When you get information from someone
(Including what and how it was said, the context and the situation)

EMOTIONS
(Reaction in terms of **feelings**)

Feelings   Beliefs

ATTITUDE

EXPERIENCE
(Reaction in terms of **beliefs**)

Behaviour

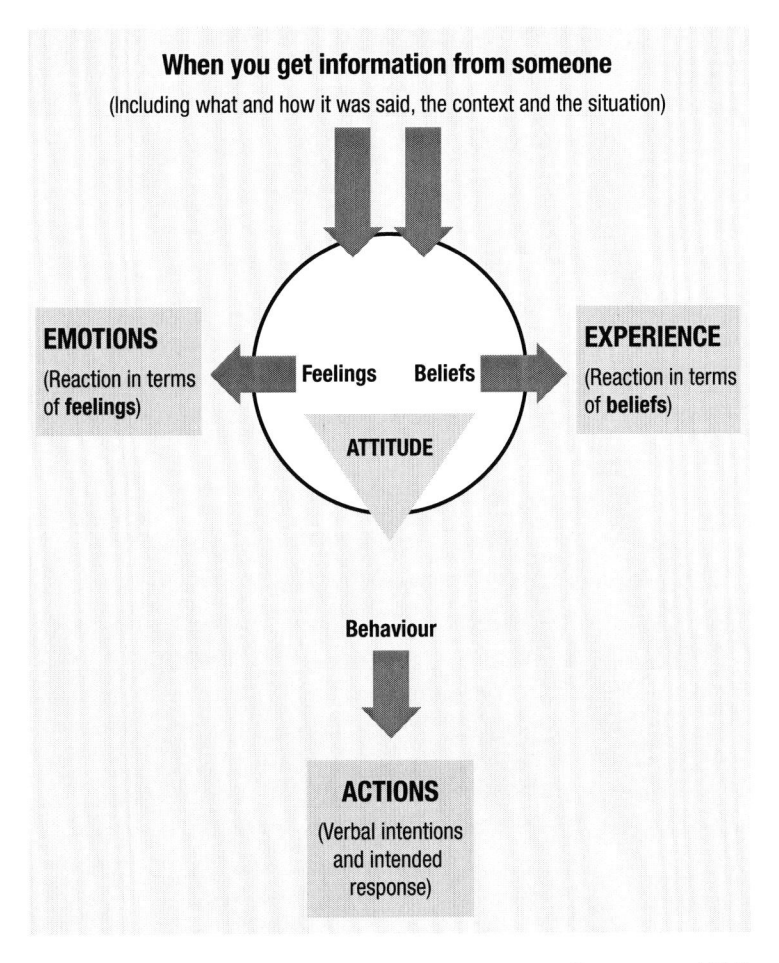

ACTIONS
(Verbal intentions and intended response)

(Spooncer 1992)

Knowing how 'attitude can affect behaviour' is important as you will need to know your sales operation's attitude towards the business objectives and targets. You will also need to know how a person feels about working with other people in the sales team.

You should compare this with your own perception. Once you understand someone's attitude you are in a better position to determine how to deal with sales-related challenges. Also, by considering how someone feels about a situation you have a better chance of improving your own decision-making.

Heider and Simmel (1944) argued that people attribute behaviour to certain causes. This then helps us make judgements about others that might be right or wrong, but once people have a certain perception it can be difficult to change. By taking the time to question how your own perception of people or a situation is arrived at, you will gain a better understanding of how and why they think and behave in the way that they do.

Adapting to change

One fundamental need for any business owner is to know how to make changes to someone's behaviour when needed. Getting the best out of people you manage often starts with the notion of 'getting the type of behaviour you are prepared to put up with!' To understand effective sales management techniques it is useful to understand aspects of *behavioural conditioning*.

If you look at the sales people you manage, there are likely to be aspects of their behaviour that you like and some that you don't like. If you identify something that needs changing you need to have a strategy of how to implement and monitor it.

You may have the authority to tell someone to change, but this is not always effective. For example, if people don't understand the change or how to do it, they might feel unable to. Other factors that can affect their ability to change include feeling threatened, unable to see the benefit or being tired of constant changes. This was referred to in Chapter 3, *Implementing your strategy (with a sales operations plan),* in the section *Preparing for change.*

This can be frustrating for you and for them! Skinner's research on *Behaviourism* (1938) is relevant to this because it focused on the consequences of certain actions. In a sales environment, by determining *what* response you are looking for, you are in a better position to create the right conditions to achieve success. Sales behaviour can be influenced by a number of factors including:

- A person's level of experience, own background, motivation and lifestyle.
- The relationship with their manager.
- The management structure.
- The culture and success of the sales operation.

Sales executives are likely to perform better if they are encouraged and rewarded. This can be done in terms of recognition, financial incentives in the form of commission and bonuses, more responsibility or the possibilities of promotion. These factors can help them to behave in a way that is in the company's best interests. However, you might not always be assertive enough to deal with potential 'conflict' situations and choose to ignore a problem!

This might sometimes seem to be the right solution, but you have to decide whether an issue is worth dealing with or not. By ignoring it, the problem often continues and becomes part of someone's everyday behaviour, which makes it harder to change. Before deciding whether to tackle a particular issue, think about the benefit of trying to solve it.

As a business owner, if there are people in your sales team (and your sales operation generally) who don't behave in a way which is acceptable, other options are available to you. These might come in the form of positive and negative reinforcement or punishment!

Reinforcement and punishment

Positive reinforcement is when you encourage a certain type of behaviour so that it will continue in the future. However, Skinner argued that there are a number of factors that stop people learning. These are particularly relevant for any sales team. They include:

- A fear of failure.
- A lack of direction and clarity.
- A lack of positive reinforcement.
- Not breaking tasks down into simple, easy to understand steps.

By understanding these elements you are in a better position to manage tasks and manage people! There are many examples of positive reinforcement in a sales environment, particularly the payment of commission and bonuses when targets have been met.

Reinforcement can also be negative. An example of this might be introducing a set of unpopular conditions on a sales team or individual, which are not lifted until a desired type of behaviour or target is achieved. In a sales context, this might include the stricter reporting of sales information, which would only be lifted once an agreed and desired outcome has been achieved.

Punishment is where someone is penalised for adopting a certain type of negative behaviour or not achieving a particular goal.

Skinner believed that punishment didn't work! He favoured positive reinforcement as an incentive to encourage the type of behaviour you want.

However, an alternative view is that punishment can work if the consequence of a repeated action is so severe that the individual doesn't repeat it. In a sales environment, this has to be put into context. Rules, such as codes of conduct, KPIs and sales targets, often determine standards of behaviour. In some situations if sales targets are repeatedly not met or rules are broken, you might feel that punishment and a disciplinary process is the best option available to you.

A comparison between these three types of conditioning can be summarised in the following way, where the outcome of a *response* is dependent on the type of conditioning that is introduced.

CONDITIONING

Positive reinforcement
Encouragement to reach a particular goal
⬇
Desired outcome = A reward and *positive situation*

Negative reinforcement
Threat to introduce a negative situation if a goal is not reached
⬇
Desired outcome = To end the *negative* situation

Punishment
Threat of a negative outcome if a desired goal is not reached
⬇
Desired result = to prevent a *negative* situation from occurring again

In summary, positive reinforcement, negative reinforcement and punishment are examples of instrumental conditioning. This is where the outcome depends upon different responses to certain predetermined types of behaviour. Understanding this is important as it will help you to know how to manage and motivate people in your sales operation.

EXERCISE

Think about how you manage people and look for examples where you have used the techniques explained earlier to change behaviour. List some examples, the approaches you used *and* the outcomes!

Examples of where you have looked to change behaviour	Method used – positive/negative reinforcement or punishment?	Outcome?
1.		
2.		
3.		

You should take time to think about the consequences of trying to change someone's behaviour in a sales environment. By doing so, you will have a better appreciation of the outcomes of your decision-making. Another way of determining sales behaviour is to look at someone's level of motivation.

Motivation

Financial remuneration is often the main measurement used as part of a sales team's motivation. Sales executives are often talked about as being highly motivated. However, financial incentives alone are not always the main drivers of an individual's motivation. For example, a young person with no responsibilities will have a different level of motivation compared to someone who is more established and experienced.

Examples of sales motivators, other than financial incentives, might include being part of a team or having the need for long-term security. Others might want self-esteem or see success as being part of a winning team. Employees normally have a desire to see their company do well and want it to have growth and stability.

It is also important to look at factors which could de-motivate people, for example:

- Not getting on with their manager or sales colleagues.
- Not feeling that they are adding value.
- Not meeting sales targets.
- Being unsure of or not liking your sales strategy or company culture.
- Feeling that they are 'carrying' other members of the sales team (by working harder or selling more).

Think about how you can get high levels of motivation from individuals and understand what motivates them. By doing this you will increase your chances of them being effective.

How your management style can improve sales performance

Intuition – unconscious influences

Every business owner constantly has to make decisions, often with time pressures. This means that you will have to rely on your intuition.

In relation to managing a sales operation, intuition can involve seeing how people react to tasks and how a sales team works together. In order to understand more about the people who work for you, look at their reactions to different situations and what might cause them to behave in a certain way. If you don't get the desired reaction to a particular request you will want to know why.

This might be explained by looking at a person's 'defence mechanisms'. This was a cornerstone of Freudian psychology and was developed by Sigmund Freud's daughter, Anna, in 1936 to describe the way in which people look to hide potentially stressful situations. For example:

Bottling things up – This involves suppressing stress when someone feels under pressure. This can be relevant where one person is not assertive and 'bottles up' their feelings. If this happens, look at how you might create an opportunity for the person to discuss his/her views.

Taking things out on someone unintentionally – This is where negative feelings are directed at someone other than the person they are really frustrated with. For example, a potential conflict at work with a figure of authority could emanate in a disagreement with someone outside of work, (a friend or relative). This might be someone who is also in a position of authority!

Blaming someone else – This is where someone's negative feelings are used to blame someone else for a particular situation (rather than admit total or partial responsibility for it). People who show this type of behaviour are often unable to consciously admit how they feel.

Solutions to these types of sales behaviour are not always easy to find. Being aware of the type of people you manage and ways in which they might repress feelings at work should help you to understand them better. This type of psychology will help you improve your management style.

Think of how you might deal with certain types of conflict situation at work. This will help you develop the confidence to make more use of your intuition and improve your managerial problem solving capability. The examples in the following table could apply to anyone in your sales operation or *you*!

EXERCISE

	Situation Someone who.....	What is a preferred solution to this situation?
1.	Doesn't communicate well with others.	
2.	Takes on too much work individually.	
3.	Is successful but not always easy to manage (or isn't a team player).	
4.	Seems to take out their frustration on a particular person in authority.	

5.	Keeps blaming someone else or picking on them.	
6.	Has personal problems which impacts on their work.	

By spending time thinking about how to solve these types of issues you will be better prepared to deal with them. Set a realistic timeframe for dealing with each one and set some time aside in your own role so that you can achieve the correct balance between leading and managing.

Leadership and management

Another challenge for many business owners is that they are often in a position of responsibility without necessarily having been specifically trained either in a sales or management role! Look at your employment history and your own strengths and weaknesses as a leader and manager and the balance between:

- Leadership – focusing on inspiring your team towards your goals.

- Management – focusing on completing the tasks to achieve those goals.

Leadership is about communicating a vision and setting an example to the people who report to you. It involves looking at how you can provide a platform for them to work well as a team. It is about delegating responsibility where appropriate and showing how a sales team in particular can work together in a motivated and unified way in order to meet the sales objectives.

Management is more focused on how tasks are carried out, for example how goals can be formulated into clearly defined actions in order to meet your sales objectives.

The balance between leadership and management is vital if you are to achieve your strategic aims. If you are the business owner, few people will question your right to lead, but being in control is not the only criteria for managing well. An example of this is if you have too much responsibility or work too hard, or if the company is not meeting its sales targets. Your management style should not be about judging people; it should focus on looking at a situation in a clear way.

If you haven't already done so, a good method of managing effectively is to formulate a *Progress and Development Plan (PDP)*. This should be reviewed at least every six months in order to look at where members of your team are at any given point in time compared to where they perceive themselves to be. You should compare this to where you want them to be, in terms of self-development.

It does require planning and does take time, but it will help you and your employees get a sense of fulfilment, understanding and direction. If you have a sales director or sales manager, this might be something that you delegate.

The importance of your perception

Understanding how your own mind processes information can also help you to ensure your intuition and perception remain as objective as possible. We all change our views from time to time, but if you are under pressure at work, a distortion can take place. This can have a negative impact on your ability to manage! To test this, here are some simple and well known examples of how your perception might differ compared to someone else!

EXERCISE

Consider the illustrations here:

In a. and b. what do you see?

In c. which is longer, the top or the bottom line?

PERCEPTUAL ILLUSIONS

Solutions to these illusions can be found at the end of this chapter.

You will often perceive a situation in a slightly different way from someone else. The challenge is how you interpret things and whether you consider someone else's point of view. This is important so that we don't stereotype people. It is supported in research carried out by Tajfel (1971) who said that people tend to over-generalise. If this happens it could affect your own decision- making capabilities.

If someone has an alternative view to you, find out why, empathise with them and look at how you can achieve a *win-win* situation. This can be challenging, especially in a sales environment.

Perhaps one of the best examples of understanding people's perception came from G Kelly (1955). He argued that people are like scientists in that we change our views depending on our experiences. He said that we test these out by either reinforcing or adapting them. By doing this we are able to re-evaluate situations and people, which will help us to make sense of our experiences.

Attributing causes to sales behaviour

Sometimes a person's attitude will cause you to take action. If so, the key to changing any type of sales behaviour at work is to:

- Try and understand someone else's point of view.
- Focus on the benefit of challenging it and trying to change it.

Looking at people's previous history and experiences when forming an opinion about them, can help you determine the best way to manage them. H. Kelley (1967) looked at this by focusing on three outcomes of behaviour in the following way:

1. Is the action common, i.e. do other people do it (e.g. turn up for internal sales meetings on time)?
2. Does the person do it regularly (e.g. turn up late for meetings)?
3. Does he/she complete other actions on time (e.g. give an up-to-date sales prospect list when asked)?

By looking at these areas you will be better able to assess whether a cause is *internal* (attributable to the individual) or *external* (attributable to the situation).

PRACTICAL EXAMPLE

If a sale is predicted one month but not achieved, a sales executive might attribute this to a prospect's situation (external reason), rather than to an inability to be realistic about the timeframe (internal reason).

By applying this type of logic you can look at whether someone's behaviour is common, repetitive and unique to the individual. By doing this you are in a better position to attribute the likely cause. If sales behaviour is common in others too, it is likely to be seen as acceptable. If it is common to the individual only, you will need to use your leadership and management skills in order to determine how to change it.

By taking the time to understand how people perceive different situations, you are more likely to gain their respect. This will help you to create good team morale and get your entire sales operation pulling in the same direction.

Chapter summary

This chapter covered two main areas:

- Understanding behaviour.
- How your management style can improve sales performance.

The key to managing people well is to understand their strengths and weaknesses. By setting a good example you will make it easier for others to 'buy in' to your decision-making. You will have some influence over how others behave which is something that needs careful consideration. It involves knowing the people you manage and motivating them to ensure you get the type of behaviour you are looking for.

In order to get the best out of your leadership and management style, you will often have to rely on your intuition as well as your sales processes. You will need to look at why a group of people think like they do in relation to team-related tasks. Their perception and yours will not always be the same. This is why you need to be adaptable in order to get the best out of your sales operation by improving your decision-making.

Key points

- ✓ Someone's attitude is an important indication of how they are likely to behave.
- ✓ Think about the outcomes you want from decisions you make.
- ✓ Try to understand why people have the views that they do in order to manage them as individuals and as a group.
- ✓ Balance being subjective and objective as part of your decision-making process.

Perceptual illusions – solutions

a. Hill (1915) – You should see one of two faces: that of an old woman or that of a young woman.

b. Rubin (1915) – You should see either a vase or two faces staring at each other.

c. Muller-Lyer illusion (1889) – Of the two *lines*, the top one looks shorter even though both lines are the same length!

Chapter 6
A strategy to manage different types of people

Chapter 6
A strategy to manage different types of people

This chapter will look at the different types of management style that can be used to implement your sales strategy. All business owners have to interact with different types of people. Having a structured approach will lead to a better style of management. The main themes focus on:

- **Management styles and forms of control.**
- **Overcoming different sales challenges.**
- **Knowing the personality types you manage.**

We will look at the ways in which you can use your management style in a positive way, including how much control to use and how much to intervene. The chapter will look at the types of challenges a sales operation faces in relation to issues which are not always easy to define and solve.

Finally, using a psychometric test can help to compare different personality types as part of an appraisal process. This will help to ensure that you understand someone's character and motivation which will improve communication within the sales team.

Management styles and forms of control

Introducing a sales strategy and setting targets often starts with a plan for sales growth defined by the senior management in a company. In determining how to implement this, the type of management style used will form a key part of how the day-to-day sales operation is run.

A business owner will have the ultimate power and operational control. However, other people might be influential depending on their:

- Role and amount of experience.
- Ability to meet the company's sales targets.
- Relationship with the business owner/other directors.

Any procedures that you implement to manage people need to be designed with a consideration of how much control to use. Business owners will sometimes delegate the day-to-day responsibility of managing a sales operation to a sales director or sales manager. This will depend on how big the company is and its structure.

It is important to think about the way you manage your sales operation, especially the sales team. Winstanley's matrix (*Power through operational influence/ownership*, 1995) looked at this in relation to how power is obtained.

There are four parts in relation to this:

1. Those whose authority is obtained through ownership of the company but who have little day-to-day influence over the running of it.
2. Those who have authority through ownership and who also exert influence over the sales operation.

3. Those who have no financial stake in the company or any authority over how the sales operation is run.
4. Those who have significant influence over the sales operation but no financial stake in the company.

The level of influence can be high or low and can be illustrated in the following way:

POWER THROUGH OPERATIONAL INFLUENCE/OWNERSHIP

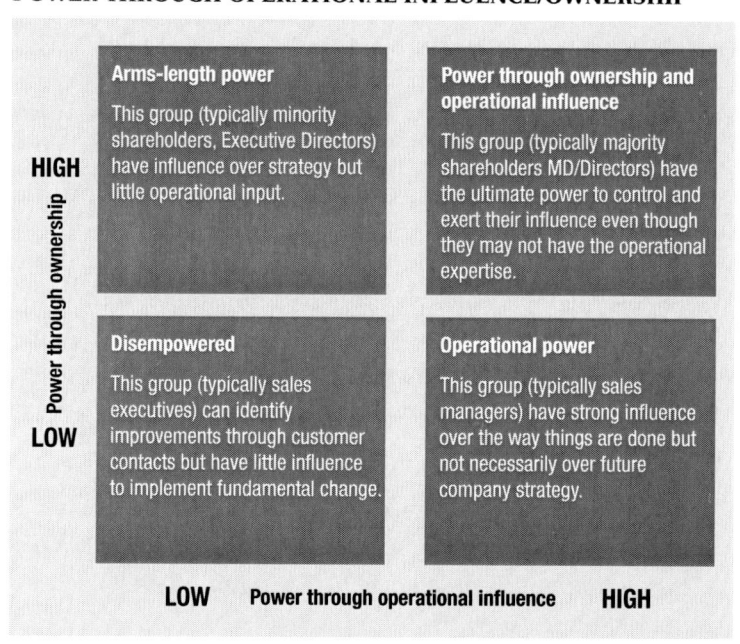

Power through ownership — HIGH / LOW
Power through operational influence — LOW / HIGH

Arms-length power (HIGH ownership, LOW operational influence)
This group (typically minority shareholders, Executive Directors) have influence over strategy but little operational input.

Power through ownership and operational influence (HIGH, HIGH)
This group (typically majority shareholders MD/Directors) have the ultimate power to control and exert their influence even though they may not have the operational expertise.

Disempowered (LOW, LOW)
This group (typically sales executives) can identify improvements through customer contacts but have little influence to implement fundamental change.

Operational power (LOW ownership, HIGH operational influence)
This group (typically sales managers) have strong influence over the way things are done but not necessarily over future company strategy.

(Winstanley et al 1995)

In many SMEs it is the business owners who influence the development of the sales operation the most. They have direct operational responsibility as well as senior management authority. A sales team's influence tends to be more informal and usually implemented at a local level. This will depend on how many employees there are and how much is delegated by the owner to other directors and managers.

If the owners keep control of many day-to-day responsibilities then they will have to deal with the issues that constantly arise from them. This has the potential to slow down decision-making and can stop a sales operation from working effectively. Another factor which will affect this is the experience of owners and their understanding of how to run a sales operation.

PRACTICAL POINTER

By ensuring that you take note of all four power groups you are more likely to design the most effective way of managing your sales operation. Remember that in most cases it is the 'disempowered' that have most contact with target accounts and customers.

The comparison between ownership and operational control can enable you to develop the most effective way of distributing power and influence. Using this model can be helpful in judging whether your sales strategy and processes work at an operational level as well as at a strategic level. To develop this, consider the three points in the following table and relate them to your own role.

EXERCISE

	Power through ownership/operational influence
1.	Complete your own matrix by identifying which groups should be placed in each segment.
2.	Identify any individuals/groups that may have too much or too little influence, which could undermine sales performance.
3.	Consider the specific needs of sales executives and how much control they might have.

By giving thought to these points you will increase your chances of understanding some of the key issues involved in making a sales operation work well. This is where a degree of flexibility and empathy is essential to allow a sales process to work for owners, directors, managers and sales executives.

You should now look at your overall approach to controlling your sales operation in relation to the different styles of sales management. This can involve loose guidelines which allow a high level of responsibility to be given to someone or tight controls which keep much of the decision-making at board level or with the business owner.

Different types of management control

The amount and type of control a business owner exercises over a sales operation can have a direct relationship with sales performance. There are four types of control, each of which will play some part in how a sales team is managed. For example:

- Direct Supervision.
- Technical Controls.

- Administrative Controls.
- Self and Social Controls.

These can be looked at in more detail.

DIRECT SUPERVISION

Direct supervision can play a large role in management control. For sales executives this might include formal end of day review meetings or regular telephone contact. Direct supervision at its most constructive can be used to look at coaching opportunities to improve someone's skills rather than just monitor that person's progress at work. However, high levels of control can be time-consuming.

TECHNICAL CONTROLS

Technical controls, such as CRM and computer systems that are designed to support the particular way that a sales operation works can also be used. These systems can monitor the numbers of entries or phone calls made by a sales team. This data can then be used for management reports. The extent to which the information is used to improve sales performance can vary greatly. Thought needs to be given about how to use the information in a constructive way.

ADMINISTRATIVE CONTROLS

These controls are achieved through formal rules, budgets, job categories and possible Human Resources (HR) procedures. They are all a form of impersonal control. For example, they can be used to manage a sales executive's progress and development or could take the form of a disciplinary procedure to manage consistent poor sales performance.

SELF AND SOCIAL CONTROLS

The structure used in some companies can rely on the individual by having informal controls in place. For example, members of a sales team may be encouraged to suggest where improvements can be made to performance. These tend to be in areas that are not closely managed. By giving individuals greater levels of responsibility to manage themselves, motivation can increase. But this might also result in risks to productivity.

It is a matter of choice that determines how tightly a sales operation is managed. This can change depending on the circumstances and the success of a preferred management style. Considering the mix of controls is essential. Having the right balance will make best use of your resources and improve your company's level of effectiveness.

The following table looks at some key questions in relation to the types of controls that often need to be in place.

EXERCISE

	Types of control	
	Questions	Answers
1.	What examples can you give of direct supervision over the people you manage?	
2.	What type of technical controls do you have?	
3.	What types of administrative controls exist?	
4.	To what extent are the sales executives (and employees in general) in control of their own daily routines?	

Any management processes in place will reflect:

- The types of product or service being offered.
- The level of trust that exists in the sales operation.
- Management skills and experience.
- The success of the current sales performance.

Being aware of the four different types of management controls gives you a choice of how to monitor your sales strategy. You might find that you naturally prefer one style over another. Or you may emphasise different types of control to people depending on the role they do. Look at adapting different styles by focusing on the challenges your company faces, its structure, culture and the types of people you manage.

PRACTICAL POINTER

The best outcome is to get the balance right in the four areas of management control. If you are too strict, you risk reducing people's level of motivation, but if there is insufficient management control in all areas, you won't get the right level of discipline in place.

Whatever processes are adopted it is important that they are implemented sensitively. Sales targets should be realistic so that they have a positive impact. This will help to maintain a high level of commitment in a sales team. If you have good discipline, processes and trust, management controls can then be loosened.

One differentiator will be the types of people who work for you. For some of those people, clear direction will be seen as a good thing. For others, a higher level of control combined with daily sales pressures can lead to misunderstandings and stress. In order to manage this, you need to understand the type of people who work for you. This involves looking at some of the sales challenges that arise and the ways in which you deal with them.

Overcoming different sales challenges

In a sales operation a combination of motivation, skills and experience will be needed to overcome any sales challenges that exist. Business owners will have to define the different types of challenges that need to be addressed. This should be followed by looking at the way in which a solution can be found to overcome a particular sales issue.

There are some key considerations to take into account, for example:

- The knowledge and experience of your sales team.
- How you sell (i.e. directly/business-to-business/over the Internet).
- The state of your market/the economy.
- The direction you want to go in.
- The resources and time at your disposal.
- The type of sales growth you are looking to achieve.

In order to make life easier for you it is worth breaking down any issue into two categories, well defined and ill defined challenges.

Planning a strategy for 'well defined' and 'ill defined' challenges

In recent years, in order to differentiate themselves, many companies have realised that *'solution selling'* is the best way to add value to a potential or existing customer. That is, looking at things from a target account/customer perspective in order to ensure that your solution best fits their needs.

This approach requires time, patience, the building of good business relationships and effective questioning skills. A consultative approach has many advantages, not least that it makes it easier to add value and to lock out the competition. It also moves away from commoditised selling in order to protect your price and profit margins. This involves different types of challenge.

A well defined challenge has four key components, featuring information about:

1. The type of challenge you are looking to solve.
2. What the goal actually is.
3. What process you intend to use to overcome the challenge.
4. The factors and restrictions that are involved in the process.

Taking this approach is very important because solving any sales issue is likely to require a structured approach.

However, what happens when the challenge is not *'well defined'*? An *'ill defined* challenge' normally involves a lack of structure, little information and a hard to identify solution. For example, where you want to achieve sales growth but you're not sure whether to improve your existing productivity or recruit new sales executives.

In sales terms, an *'ill defined'* challenge will need the person solving it to help define the sales issue. When applying this to developing sales revenue it would involve knowing the target account's decision-making process, products/services and needs. This will mean taking a structured approach and being skilled in:

- Exploring any issues.
- Looking at the effect on the company you are targeting.
- Ensuring that the target account/customer actually thinks an issue is worth solving.
- Providing the right solution.

If you assume that all challenges can be easily defined or are always solvable, you limit the possible options and strategies available to you. In some cases if target accounts are not easy to sell to or a market is not easy to break into, you will need to be creative when finding a suitable solution.

Thinking outside the box

One of the best examples of illustrating an *'ill defined'* challenge and then having a strategy for solving it was put forward by Scheerer (1963). His interpretation was from an earlier illustration of the *Nine Dot Problem* (Loyd 1914).

It highlights how looking at something from different perspectives can improve your objectivity and help you to look at alternative solutions to common sales challenges. It is a good example *of lateral thinking*. This requires a need to use ideas that are not always obvious and which can often be solved by thinking in a creative manner.

The following exercise (which may be familiar) requires you to draw four continuous straight lines on a piece of paper illustrated with nine dots. Pass the lines through each dot in the process *without* taking your pen off the page! You can start anywhere you choose. See if you can do it!

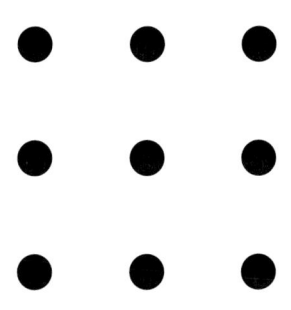

•   •   •

•   •   •

•   •   •

An example of how this *'problem'* can be solved can be seen at the end of this chapter. One of the main reasons it isn't easy to solve is the lack of prior knowledge. In selling terms, you cannot always overcome a challenge by assuming that it is the same as another, even if it looks similar to something you have solved in the past.

There are two key points here in relation to problem solving and managing a sales team:

1. Challenges require some thought and planning *before* any action can be taken.
2. Just because you perceive a challenge in a certain way doesn't mean that someone else will.

This last point may be particularly difficult for some business owners to accept. If you own the company then you are expected to give direction and leadership. But this has to be countered by involving your colleagues and taking their ideas and strategies into account. By being aware of this you are in a better position to be more objective. However, this will require respect for alternative approaches, especially if they differ from your own.

It is essential to know what type of people you are managing and how they perceive sales challenges. To develop this further, the focus will now be on how psychometric tests can be used to help understand a sales person's character and motivation. They can also test someone's preferred way of dealing with 'well defined' and 'ill defined' sales challenges.

Knowing the personality types you manage

Identifying positive sales traits

Many business owners might not consider using a psychometric test as a way of establishing a sales executive's personality traits. However, in order to understand the type of personality someone has you should consider this test as part of an appraisal process.

Many modern day models used to interview sales people stem from Eysenck's *Type Theory* (1947), which was a development from earlier trait theories. In selling terms *Type Theory* can be used to cover different types of behaviour in two opposing ways:

1. Stability versus instability.
2. Extrovert versus introvert.

No psychometric test is 100% accurate but it can be very useful in a sales environment. A typical breakdown of traits might include looking at testing a person's attitude towards punctuality, reliability and self-discipline, and how outgoing or people-focused someone is.

This was pioneered by Cattell and Kline (1977) who looked to measure the relevant personality traits of someone who could be:

- Affected by feelings (i.e. submissive or apprehensive).
- Tough minded.
- Trusting and self-assured.
- Group orientated.
- Relaxed.
- Enthusiastic and imaginative.
- Self-sufficient.

The questions in many psychometric tests require that you look at four words and then select the one that you identify with most closely.

Assessing your personality traits

You can also use a personality test as part of your interview process. If you have a better understanding of the type of people you employ, you will be in a better position to manage them well. This will make them more effective, which will maximise your investment in them. By doing this you are likely to get more out of them in terms of effort and reward.

In relation to your own communication with others:

- Have you ever wondered what type of characteristics you have?
- Have you looked at any of your sales executive's motivators (other than financial remuneration)?
- How aware are you of factors affecting your ability to manage a sales operation?

In order to find out, complete this simple test.

Don't try and analyse the words too much!

It should take no more than 5 minutes!

There are no right or wrong answers. Don't spend more than a few seconds on your choice of answer for each question. Finally, be honest, don't try and second guess the potential outcome of the test, this way it will be more realistic!

STEP 1

Opposite is a table; look at the first row and pick the word that *you* identify with most or best describes you. Choose the word that most describes *you*. Then write down your choice of A, B, C, or D. For example, in question 1, if you pick 'Fun', put B in the answer box (in the far right column). Carry on until all 20 questions have been answered.

PERSONALITY TEST

Q	A	B	C	D	Answer
1.	Commitment	Fun	Objectives	People	
2.	Tolerance	Order	Free	Respect	
3.	Organise	Meeting	Talk	Party	
4.	Precision	Popular	Win	Kind	
5.	Leadership	Friendship	Intellectual	Management	
6.	Self-esteem	Structure	Teamwork	Control	
7.	Patience	Decision	Delay	Laugh	
8.	Functional	Complex	Partnership	Agenda	
9.	Sure	Procedure	Artistic	Empathy	
10.	Subjective	Tolerance	Right	Wrong	
11.	Together	Focus	Development	Outgoing	
12.	Suppress	Avoid	Emotional	Confront	
13.	Cross	Unreliable	Impatience	Sympathetic	
14.	Feelings	Understanding	Proper	Simple	
15.	On time	Punishment	Withdraw	Late	
16.	Listen	Boredom	Sensitive	Fast	
17.	Agreement	Opinion	Finish	Relationship	
18.	Talk	Group	Strong	Fact	
19.	Completed	Firm	Rush	Reliable	
20.	Partner	Outgoing	Fixed	Indecision	

STEP 2

Now look at the following table which will relate to your answers. From this you can find out how to complete your score!

THE ANSWERS

Q	Control	Extrovert	Procedure	People
1.	A	B	D	C
2.	D	C	B	A
3.	B	D	A	C
4.	C	B	A	D
5.	A	C	D	B
6.	D	A	B	C
7.	C	D	B	A
8.	A	B	D	C
9.	A	C	B	D
10.	B	D	C	A
11.	B	D	C	A
12.	D	C	A	B
13.	A	C	B	D
14.	D	A	C	B
15.	B	C	A	D
16.	C	D	B	A
17.	B	A	C	D
18.	C	A	D	B
19.	B	C	A	D
20.	D	B	C	A

STEP 3

Complete the marking by giving yourself one point only in the relevant row until all 20 questions have been marked. Then add up the number of marks you have in each COLUMN. You should then have a number in the 'final score' row below for each of the four primary traits.

Q	Control	Extrovert	Procedure	People
1.				
2.				
3.				
4.				
5.				
6.				
7.				
8.				
9.				
10.				
11.				
12.				
13.				
14.				
15.				
16.				
17.				
18.				
19.				
20.				
Final score				

Now refer back to which of the four primary traits you have scored the most in, i.e. find out where your main focus lies. A highest score in:

Column A = Primary focus is on *CONTROL*

Column B = Primary focus is on being an *EXTROVERT*

Column C = Primary focus is on *PROCEDURE*

Column D = Primary focus is on *PEOPLE*

So, if someone has *Control* as the primary focus, for example, he/she will have strong characteristics of self-reliance. However, in extreme circumstances, this person might come across as aggressive. Similarly, each of the other three primary areas of focus will have their common characteristics and traits.

These four personality types can be summarised to highlight their interaction with each other. The following example illustrates the main positive characteristics of someone who has a particularly high score in one of the personality type areas. It also shows the potentially negative behaviour this personality type may resort to (especially under pressure).

PERSONALITY TYPES

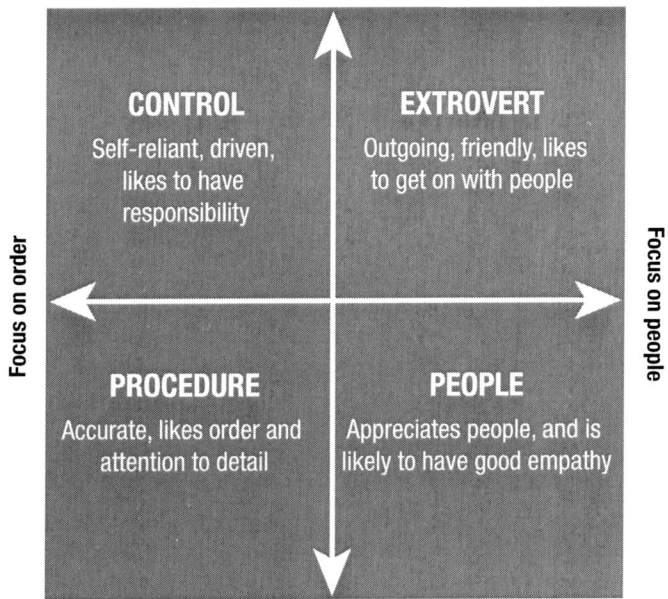

Extremes can lead to someone being
aggressive or over **confident**

Focus on order

CONTROL
Self-reliant, driven, likes to have responsibility

EXTROVERT
Outgoing, friendly, likes to get on with people

PROCEDURE
Accurate, likes order and attention to detail

PEOPLE
Appreciates people, and is likely to have good empathy

Focus on people

Extremes can lead to someone being
defensive or **submissive**

An ideal outcome would be where the scores are fairly even. This indicates a balanced approach to problem solving. It also shows a degree of flexibility and contrast between one behavioural type and another.

Being strong in one particular area is not necessarily a problem. Many business owners look for sales executives to be outgoing, self-reliant and extrovert. But it is good to be aware when someone might come across these boundaries, i.e. aggressive or over confident.

In order to manage this, look at some of the disadvantages of extreme characteristics in the following table:

CONCERNS (of someone with extreme personality types)
CONTROL
• May come across as aggressive. • Won't always listen. • Not always a team player/may challenge authority.
EXTROVERT
• May miss deadlines. • Can be defensive when challenged. • Can appear over confident.
PROCEDURE
• May rely on structure to be effective. • Can become too focused on process. • Can lose interest if procedures are not followed.
PEOPLE
• May become submissive if challenged. • Not always open to new ideas. • May be too worried about people's feelings.

Having a good understanding of the primary personality characteristics of people in a sales team (and in a sales operation generally) will help you to manage them better. However, there are limitations to using a psychometric test.

Limitations of using psychometric tests

Any psychometric test can have flaws – there can be questions over their reliability. Some people might be nervous about completing one or give the answers they think you want, rather than those they would normally choose. For example, in Question 3 they might choose the word *'Organise' (A)* because they think it is the right image to project, while not wanting to admit to *not* being very well organised.

Another criticism of psychometric tests is that they can be rigid and don't take into account other dimensions of someone's personality, like their situation or experience.

Similarly, psychometric tests have been criticised for describing but not explaining someone's personality! They can give an indication as to how someone thinks but not how this can be adapted to different selling situations.

However, the outcome of tests like this can have good learning points particularly as part of an appraisal process. They can help to support your subjective views of someone. With this in mind, it is a good idea to have a discussion with employees about the results of any test. This might include discussing whether the person agrees with the results and, if so, how that might relate to the job they are doing.

Whatever their limitations, psychometric tests can give another dimension to successfully managing a sales operation. Developing people in a sales role can be a costly investment and any means of helping with this is beneficial.

Chapter summary

This chapter covered three main areas:

- Management styles and forms of control.
- Overcoming different sales challenges.
- Knowing the personality types you manage.

In order to achieve your goals ensure that you have the right level of control in your processes. Plan a sales strategy based on how well you can define potential challenges and look at different types of solutions. Identifying these will help you overcome any difficulties when implementing the strategy.

Finally, in order to help your employees meet these challenges, consider using a psychometric test to assist you. It involves understanding the personality traits of the people in your sales operation. This will help any business owner to adapt to different types of character and to manage them well.

Key points

- ✓ Think about the amount of power you have as a business owner and how this can be put to good use in a positive way.
- ✓ Consider the type of sales management style and controls you have and how suited they are to the day-to-day running of your company.
- ✓ Remember to define the sales challenges you face in order to provide appropriate solutions.
- ✓ Consider the benefits of using psychometric tests as a part of your sales development process.

Answer to the *Nine Dot Problem*

Many people find this problem difficult to solve because they perceive the nine dots as a square or box! However, this limits our ability to solve it, as there is an assumption that the lines have to stay inside a perceived box, which is formed by the dots.

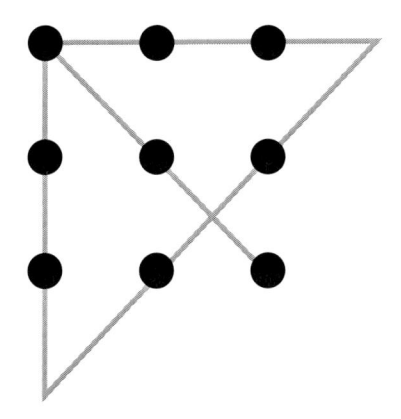

This is one of several ways to solve the *'problem'* depending on where you start (which in this example was the bottom right hand dot). To solve it requires you to think *'outside the box'* (which is where this well-known phrase came from)!

Chapter 7
Teamwork and communication

Chapter 7
Teamwork and communication

Teamwork and having effective communication skills are important factors in getting the best out of your sales operation. This involves understanding an individual's decision-making process and communication style. This chapter looks at:

- **Working as part of a team.**
- **Being assertive.**
- **Communication skills.**

Successful sales performance is underpinned by how well your entire sales operation works together. Business owners need to get the most out of the people they employ. This can be helped by understanding the difference between assertive, passive and aggressive behaviour. A questionnaire can be used to test your own level of assertiveness and that of the people in your sales operation.

This has a strong link with the need for good communication skills because conflict at work can have a negative impact on the company. This is why finding a positive way to communicate can save you time and increase productivity. It will also promote good internal and external business relationships, all of which are vital if you are to implement your sales strategy well.

Working as part of a team

Understanding a person's individual decision-making

Before you can understand how to motivate a sales team, look at the type of people you are managing. Look at how well they work together to meet your sales objectives and how this compares with their own goals.

This can be described using Neumann and Morgenstern's *Game Theory* (1944). Primarily, it looked at the best strategy for an individual by taking into account how the person you are talking to might react. It is concerned with self-interest and making use of the information available to achieve the best possible outcome, or the nearest someone can get to this.

It is based on making choices and the consequences that follow. It looks at the balance of conflict and co-operation between people in relation to tactics and decision-making. By predicting an outcome correctly it will help you make good decisions.

The *Prisoners Dilemma* (Powers 1988) helps to support *Game Theory*. This is when two prisoners have been questioned separately about whether they have committed a crime. They have a choice: confess, and by doing so implicate the other, or deny and hope that their accomplice does the same. If they confess they will both get a sentence but it will be less than if one confesses and the other does not. If both deny they will be free to go. The question is, what is the best option for each prisoner?

In relation to a sales team, *Game Theory* examines how someone makes decisions based on two options: to accept something or reject it. If you look at two people (or groups), this can create the following types of scenarios:

- *Win–Win*
- *Win–Lose*
- *Lose–Win*
- *Lose-Lose*

This can be applied to internal relationships (sales executives and sales management) or external business relationships.

Not everyone will have the same level of motivation to achieve your sales objectives. This means that as a business owner you need to give consideration to your decision-making and the implications this can have for a sales team and the sales operation.

PRACTICAL EXAMPLE

Imagine that a team target is introduced with shared team bonuses. Even if the majority of sales executives 'buy in' to this, those who don't might not say so if they are in a minority. If these people were earning more on individual targets they might decide to use alternative strategies to avoid confrontation.

This might include working less hard, being disruptive or planning to leave the company. This will have consequences in the future for the individual and for the sales team.

Often, knowing a person's real intentions can be hard to predict if that person doesn't completely 'buy in' to the company's sales strategy. In a sales team, you often have some strong personalities. This means that each person will have their own preferences of how things should be done and how to meet individual sales targets. This will still apply even if you have agreed standards and procedures in place.

This is relevant to managing people in a sales role because it will help business owners to better understand a sales executive's decision-making process. This applies when management objectives need to be interpreted and implemented by a sales team in the same way, in order to ensure that they work well together.

How well changes are introduced will also depend on the strength of the relationship between the business owner (as well as a sales director or sales manager) and members of the team.

Understanding individual and group decision-making will put you in a better position to predict and manage sales behaviour. This will make it easier to communicate with team members in order to maximise each person's sales performance.

If members of a sales team are receptive to your sales strategy then they are likely to be co-operative in helping to make it work. But if they don't see the benefit you may find that even though they appear to implement the strategy, you might see examples of people not 'buying in' to it. This will have negative consequences in terms of sales performance and team morale.

Game Theory is relevant to how members of a sales team think because it looks at understanding and predicting their behaviour. This is helpful for anyone managing in a competitive sales environment.

Being a team player

It is the nature of most sales executives to be highly motivated and enthusiastic, and to be able to form strong business relationships. Having good social skills is a vital part of that.

Being a team player might seem to contradict to some extent the need for someone who is driven and focused. However, if a team ethic isn't installed in a sales operation it can affect your performance. It can also lead to:

- Customer complaints.
- A lack of co-operation within a team.
- Poor account management development.
- Internal conflict between colleagues.

These types of examples waste time and resources and make it more difficult to reach your sales targets. Some issues could be resolved with better internal discipline, but others are not always possible to change easily. In order to ensure that your sales operation is working well, consider the following measures to help maintain successful team principles:

- Remind employees of their team responsibilities (as well as ones which focus more on the individual aspects of their role).
- Look at ways of encouraging regular contact and co-operation between sales executives and other internal departments.
- Set up a code of conduct including individual *Personal Development Plans* (PDPs).
- Encourage a 'can do' approach.
- Set up internal team meetings and incentives that involve different parts of the sales operation.

The last thing any business owner wants is for internal conflict to affect the potential success of the company.

The appropriate use of language

Another element that can affect internal and external business relationships is language! This might sound obvious but communication with colleagues (and some customers) is likely to be more informal than with buyers in new target accounts. This familiarisation can be good for team interaction. However, internally, it can sometimes lead to people not maintaining a high level of discipline or showing the level of respect that should be afforded to a manager or customer.

One way to counter this is to encourage sales executives (and everyone else in the sales operation) to treat colleagues as 'internal' customers. By encouraging people to have empathy and be constructive, you increase the chances of good team communication.

As a business owner, levels of assertiveness and levels of expectation need to be defined. As far as communication with customers is concerned, it is important to be aware of a number of things:

- The job role and level of seniority of the customer.
- The relationship and level of trust you have with your customers.
- The way in which you sell your products and services.
- An employee's job role and level of experience.
- Your internal procedures and training methods.

Common sense and good social skills will help determine the type of language and communication that should be used. But you should encourage people in your sales operation to:

- Avoid 'over familiarity' with customers.
- Do what they say, i.e. be consistent.
- Avoid confrontation.
- Listen (when engaging in a conversation).

Don't confuse customer service skills (which are largely reactive), with selling skills (which are more pro-active). Effective communication can be improved by finding out what customers want and how they like to be treated.

Group sales behaviour

Some of the questions that arise from this type of discussion include what makes people get on with some people and not others. Group behaviour forms part of the sales culture which was looked at in Chapter 1, *Responding to changes in the market,* in the section *Adapting a company's sales culture*.

Some of the most important research in this area was done by Tajfel (1971), in his *Social Identity Theory*. He showed how a group could take on a social identity by sharing common identification. This can be termed as an *'in-group'*, as opposed to an *'out-group'* (which doesn't take on a social identity). He found that being part of a particular group can give a person a sense of belonging by creating a feeling of well-being.

Tajfel's research showed that by categorising individuals into groups, a certain degree of prejudice would occur. This is sometimes common in a competitive sales environment.

This is relevant to group interaction and should be looked at from an internal and external perspective. For example, internally, a sales team might see a service team as an *'out-group'* by not sharing the same goals or having the same level of pressure or responsibilities as they perceive they have (or vice versa). This can present challenges for business owners and is a key reason why internal communication is a vital part of leadership and management skills.

If you sell commodity products or services a customer or a supplier can often be seen as the *'out-group'*. It may be difficult to eliminate this type of behaviour altogether. But the potential consequences of seeing customers as too demanding can be extremely damaging. It is something that a business owner should monitor and control.

Now think about different parts of your own sales operation and look for examples of where you have witnessed potential conflict. Then look at possible solutions you could put in place.

EXERCISE

What is the potential conflict issue?	Which area and with whom does the issue lie with?	What possible solutions could you put in place?
1. Example		
Orders are taken without consideration to the service department's ability to deliver them.	Sales team and service department. Issue for sales and service managers.	Arrange a meeting to improve the management of the sales pipeline.
2.		
3.		

This is why working well as a team is a vital part of a sales operation being able to achieve their sales goals. In relation to this, look at how people relate to each other so that you get to know an individual's behaviour. Byrne and Core introduced their *Reinforcement-Affect Theory* (1970), which suggested that we tend to like people who are positive towards us and dislike those who are negative towards us. Understanding this can help you manage people better.

It's important to look at how individuals relate to each other, which is often based on:

- If they know the other person.
- If they like the other person.
- How well someone they know and like gets on with a particular person.

A good or bad personal relationship with someone at work can affect another person's attitude. This is an important element in promoting team behaviour and developing good business relationships with target accounts and customers.

Working hard and working effectively

Another part of getting the best out of people is to ensure that they don't become over-worked. For sales executives, exceeding sales targets on a regular basis requires discipline and often long working hours.

Perhaps a greater challenge is when sales executives are unaware of how hard they are working and become tired and at times ineffective. This is particularly apparent in the following circumstances:

- When someone starts showing signs of stress and irritability.
- When someone is not reaching the sales targets.
- When their performance affects other people in the sales operation.

In this situation it can be difficult to be objective and to take the necessary steps to reduce someone's workload (including your own)! As a business owner, much of the responsibility for your company's success and for managing people well, will lie with you. If you feel under pressure at work, look at how you could delegate work to someone else.

If you continue ignoring the signs of overwork it will affect your ability to get the most out of yourself and the people you manage. This is likely to have a negative impact on your sales performance and will stop you from being as effective as you could be. To avoid this, ensure that you get the balance right between working hard and working effectively. This is covered in Chapter 8, *Working more productively*.

Being assertive

As a business owner you should have the respect of the people who work for you. However, in any competitive and potentially high pressure sales environment there can be times when people react to situations in different ways. Some can become defensive, others aggressive and some people will want to avoid conflict altogether.

You should set boundaries for what is and what isn't acceptable behaviour, and look to earn respect by being assertive in your leadership style.

Assessing your level of assertiveness

In order to test your own level of assertiveness, complete the following questionnaire. You can also ask other people in your sales operation to complete it. Answer the questions by circling the number that best describes you. Be as honest as possible and when you have finished, you can assess your score.

Answers:
0 = No
1 = Occasionally
2 = Often
3 = Yes

Assertiveness questionnaire

1.	Can you say no to an unreasonable request?	0	1	2	3
2.	If you are annoyed with someone do you tend to avoid that person and a potential confrontation?	0	1	2	3
3.	If you receive something from a colleague that is below a certain standard, do you ask them to correct it?	0	1	2	3
4.	If you think something is important during a conversation, do you interrupt the other person?	0	1	2	3
5.	Do you ever find it hard to maintain eye contact when you are talking to a colleague?	0	1	2	3
6.	Do you have confidence in decisions you make at work?	0	1	2	3
7.	Do you find it difficult to compliment other people?	0	1	2	3
8.	In a meeting, do you keep your views to yourself with people who are more experienced than you?	0	1	2	3
9.	If you disagree with someone you respect, do you tell that person?	0	1	2	3
10.	Do you think of ways of getting back at people who have annoyed you?	0	1	2	3
11.	Do you have to have the last word in a conversation?	0	1	2	3
12.	If you need help with a particular situation, do you ask for it?	0	1	2	3
13.	Do you feel uncomfortable if someone compliments you at work?	0	1	2	3
14.	Do you become defensive if someone appears to be criticising you in some way?	0	1	2	3
15.	Are you conscious of behaving in a way that you think other people want you to?	0	1	2	3
16.	If someone is late in sending you information that was promised to you, do you tell that person?	0	1	2	3
17.	Do you tend to ignore the opinions of colleagues who are less senior than you?	0	1	2	3
18.	Do you tend to go along with things, i.e. 'anything for a quiet life'?	0	1	2	3

ASSERTIVENESS ASSESSMENT – SCORES

To complete your assessment, look at the following table and put in the number you scored for each question in the relevant Score column. Continue until you have a score for each question. Then add up the total points assigned in each of the three columns to complete your assertiveness profile.

ASSERTIVENESS SCORE TABLE

Question	Score	Question	Score	Question	Score
1.		2.		4.	
3.		5.		7.	
6.		8.		10.	
9.		13.		11.	
12.		15.		14.	
16.		18.		17.	
TOTAL →		TOTAL →		TOTAL →	
Assertive		Passive		Aggressive	

You might think that an ideal score would be 18 points for Assertiveness and 0 points for Passive and Aggressive. However, a score of between 12 and 18 for Assertiveness would be considered good.

If there is a score of less than 12 in the assertiveness category, re-look at the questions and consider what stops you (or the person doing the test) behaving in an assertive way and what you can do to address this.

If there is a score of 9 or over in the passive or aggressive categories, look at ways to be more assertive. Go back to the questionnaire and reassess the other options available. Then compare the answer given to the assertiveness option for that particular question.

If there is a score of 12 or more in the assertiveness category, but a score of 9 or more in the passive or aggressive category you need to ask yourself why. This could indicate that you (or the person doing the test) resorts to one of two more extreme types of communication when put under pressure. Look at what you can do to address this so that an assertive manner can be maintained in order to achieve positive communication with others.

Remember that no one is likely to be assertive all of the time.

Comparing aggressive, passive and assertive behaviour

In order to understand and manage different types of people at work, it is worth defining the three main categories of behaviour which have been highlighted.

Aggressive behaviour often creates a *Win-Lose* situation. This is when someone gets what he/she wants without thinking about another person's position or feelings. This can lead to the person who loses feeling humiliated, frustrated or de-motivated.

Passive behaviour can create a *Lose-Win* situation. This is when one person gives in by not standing up for themselves. It is when someone doesn't want to confront a situation and that person feels that his/her views are not appreciated (or even ignored).

Assertive behaviour creates a *Win-Win* situation. With this outcome, both parties are more open and responsive to listening and working with each other to achieve the desired result. People go away feeling satisfied and valued.

PRACTICAL POINTER

Be aware that it is not always what you say but how you say it that people will remember in your communication with them (and vice versa). This is why you need to think about how you come across to people, particularly when you or they are under pressure.

A *win-win* outcome should be the ideal for everyone to aim for in standards of communication with others.

It is important to be assertive, as it will help you to:

- Get your views across while respecting someone else's.
- Lessen the chance of conflict.
- Gain someone else's respect.
- Maintain positive relations with others.

One challenging issue can be how to react when people are aggressive towards you! If you respond either passively or aggressively you are more likely to see an outcome which neither person is entirely happy with. If this type of communication reoccurs it is more likely that resentment will become apparent and a pattern for future communication set.

That is why if you get into a discussion with someone who behaves in either a passive or aggressive way, maintain a sensitive but assertive approach. You will need to have good listening skills and empathy with some people in order to ensure that each person comes away feeling that a positive outcome was achieved. Ideally this would apply even if one person isn't pleased with the actual point which was being discussed.

Now we will look at how you change your type of communication in order to maintain assertive behaviour for both parties.

Communication skills

Looking at how people in a sales operation interact with each other can help business owners to understand the best way for them to work together. Sometimes however, misunderstandings and potential conflict can arise.

If this happens, find out why communication has broken down between people at work and what the causes could be. The answers to this often lie in a number of key areas, particularly for people who:

- Work too hard or are under-performing.
- Have unrealistic work expectations or have a fear of failure.
- Are unhappy with their home life.
- Have different work agendas from colleagues.
- Lack empathy with other departments and other people.
- Have not been trained well enough in their role.

Whatever the reasons for potential conflict, you can't be expected to have all of the answers to resolve them. Nor can you expect to examine all of the causes. Some of these will lie within the individual and some in the work processes they have been asked to follow.

To get the most out of people working together, make sure that each person knows what is expected of them in their job role and set them boundaries in relation to this. Ensure that you set out what you expect from people in a fair and manageable way, and note goals that were or were not achieved. You should also look at how this fits in with the company's overall sales performance and business goals.

You can also introduce a *'code of conduct' to* minimise the chances of conflict arising. Most people who are focused on being positive and are highly motivated will want to avoid conflict. It is a challenge for any business owner to install disciplines that maximise the chances of managing people well.

Communicating in a positive way

There are times when, in a high-pressure sales environment, customers and colleagues will feel under stress. This can lead to a breakdown in communication and frustration from both sides. If this is not managed well it can lead to trends in sales behaviour that can be difficult to change.

Research done by Eric Berne in the late 1950s helped to illustrate how different types of communication affected social and business relationships. He called this *Transactional Analysis* (TA) and showed how people can communicate with each other in the most positive way. This was later developed in a book entitled *Games People Play* (1964).

This is particularly relevant for any manager of a sales team because it defines three preferred states that people tend to use when talking to each other. It also shows how to adapt your style to ensure positive communication can take place. Berne compared interaction between people to a game people play in order to get their own way.

He said that these games give us a sense of control and identity, and also reassure us. This involves strategies, which are used to maximise the chances of a *Win–Win* outcome. Examples of this might include formal business greetings or a conversation where we take different positions for different types of meeting (which can be positive or negative). This gives us a sense of control and identity.

Sales executives will, to some extent, have their own agenda and strategy in relation to their role. As a business owner you will have yours, just as customers will have theirs.

Berne argued that communication could be controlled and managed. His research focused on three main *'Ego states'* that people use to communicate with others:

1. *Parent* – This involves an example of a nurturing parent, who is positive or one that spoils a child which is seen as negative.

2. *Adult* – This is the preferred state as it involves compromise. The *Adult* state represents someone who is comfortable with whom he or she is.

3. *Child* – This involves a co-operative child, who is positive and compliant or a resistant child, which is seen as negative.

This can be illustrated in the following way:

TRANSACTIONAL ANALYSIS

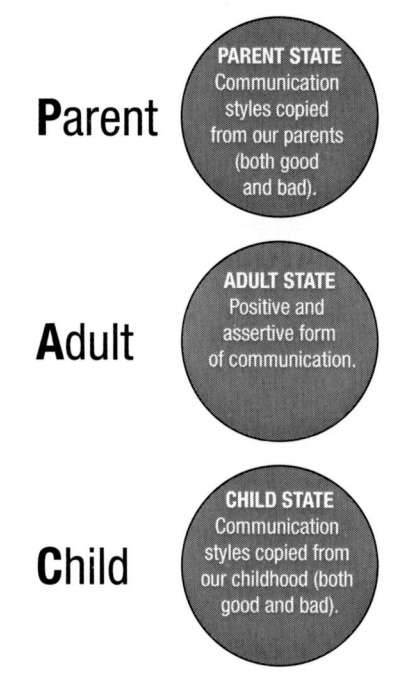

Parent — **PARENT STATE** Communication styles copied from our parents (both good and bad).

Adult — **ADULT STATE** Positive and assertive form of communication.

Child — **CHILD STATE** Communication styles copied from our childhood (both good and bad).

(Berne)

By understanding *Transactional Analysis* and applying it, you and any group of people you manage will be in a better position to communicate well with each other, as well as target accounts and customers.

In the following illustration you can see the different types of communication style that could be adopted by two people – the preferred style being *Adult to Adult (A-A)*. In this state both people are communicating on the same level. This means that they have the best chance of interacting well by listening and having respect for each other.

TYPES OF PARENT, ADULT, CHILD COMMUNICATION

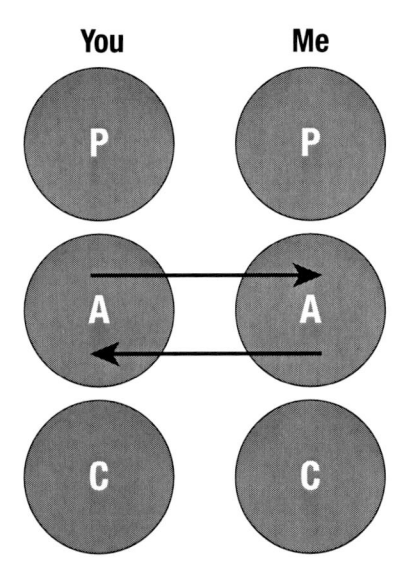

(Berne 1964)

Potential conflict can occur when communication transactions are crossed, i.e. when you or the other person is on a different communication level. This is often because different styles of communication can lead to misunderstandings.

Transactional Analysis does not imply that you ever see employees or customers as parents or children! But sometimes, behaviour can mirror one of these states; that is what Byrne was trying to illustrate. When this happens, he said that by maintaining an *Adult* state, there was more chance that the other person would be likely to respond in that *Adult* state. This might avoid the 'overly dominant parent' and 'submissive child' position.

If you remain assertive and have empathy for someone else, there is more chance that they will behave in the same way towards you. This will help to ensure that both parties are in the best position to get the most out of any conversation.

Looking for a win-win outcome

Another way of expressing the *Parent, Adult, Child* concept is to consider whether *you* and the person you are communicating with will achieve a positive outcome. This can be summarised as *I'm OK, you're OK* (Harris 1967), and can be illustrated in the following way:

I'M OK, YOU'RE OK

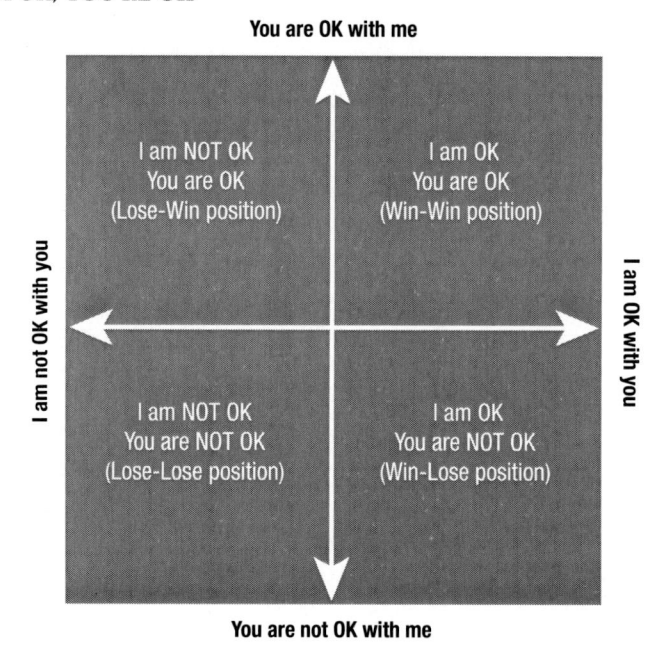

You are OK with me

	I am OK with you
I am NOT OK / You are OK / (Lose-Win position)	I am OK / You are OK / (Win-Win position)
I am NOT OK / You are NOT OK / (Lose-Lose position)	I am OK / You are NOT OK / (Win-Lose position)

I am not OK with you ← → I am OK with you

You are not OK with me

(Harris 1967)

This example shows how communication can break down unless both people feel happy with the outcome. Taking the time to look at something from another person's point of view will help to create a *Win–Win* situation.

Perfecting communication skills takes time and patience. However, it will improve your business relationships, as well as those with suppliers, customers and target accounts.

Chapter summary

This chapter covered three main areas:

- Working as part of a team.
- Being assertive.
- Communication skills.

It is essential that you look at how you and your sales operation work together in order to get the most out of their efforts. This will involve them and you being assertive and having empathy with other people.

Having good communication skills will improve your chances of implementing your sales strategy successfully. This will make the goals and targets easier to achieve, and help you to create a positive environment at work.

Key points

✓ Get to know the different types of people in your sales operation in order to get the best out of them.

✓ Encourage people to be assertive to reduce the chances of them demonstrating aggressive or passive behaviour.

- ✓ Identify potential causes of conflict at work so they can be resolved.
- ✓ Take time to think about how you and your employees communicate with people to create a *Win–Win* outcome.

**Chapter 8
Working more productively**

Chapter 8
Working more productively

Business relationships at work encourage people to pull together to create an effective and motivational sales environment. This chapter looks at your own approach to work, that of the people in your sales operation, and the areas which impact on them. It includes:

- **Work/life balance.**
- **Roles and responsibilities.**

Having a balance between work and home life will help to increase a business owner's productivity. However, inevitably, managing a company can generate long hours and pressures associated with ensuring that sales targets are met. This can lead to stress which needs to be managed to ensure that you remain positive and effective.

When you are managing internal business relationships, there can be an over reliance on some members of staff. This can happen if a person has too much influence on the sales process or a sales team. To improve your (and your employees) *work/life balance* the chapter emphasises the importance of the roles and responsibilities of people in a sales operation.

Work/life balance

Living with the pressure of everyday life

In a sales operation, working long hours is a normal part of many people's daily routine. This often means that they might not always have as much time to spend on their home lives as they would like. However, a more stress free environment can often be achieved by looking at the quantity and the quality of work everyone does, (especially a business owner).

People in a sales role can also feel the effects of being under pressure, which is why it is good to encourage them to look at ways to strike the right balance between their work and home life.

It is important to feel that your job doesn't compromise your home life (possibly to the extent where you don't even feel that you have a home life!).

In a smaller company, business owners and people in sales roles have to be adaptable as there is often a less structured environment compared to a large company. In order to understand your own work/life balance and how to manage it, consider these questions:

EXERCISE

1. What pressures do you get at work?
   -
   -
   -

2. What do you like about your job role?
   -
   -
   -

3. What don't you like about your job role?
   -
   -
   -

You might want to think about the impact of your answers on you and your employees! Being aware of how you manage yourself will help you to be more objective.

Managing long hours

As we have said many business owners work long hours and expect people in their sales operation to do the same. Dedication, staff shortages and a desire to 'get the job done' are often given as reasons for this.

Some companies have flexible policies to alleviate long hours; for example, working from home. Others may not trust a sales executive to do this.

In many customer facing sales roles, there can be a large amount of travelling. That is why it is worth considering how sales performance can be managed if someone lives many miles from their nearest office.

Too much focus on work ethic can be misleading and sometimes counter-productive. Gorz (2005) argued that the work ethic has become obsolete. 'It is no longer true that producing more means working more, or that producing more will lead to a better way of life'. This can have implications in relation to the quality of work someone produces.

'Working smarter, not harder' is a well-known phrase often used to describe focusing on being more effective. But it isn't always adhered to in times of pressure or poor sales, or in an economic downturn. To focus more on this, complete the following exercise:

EXERCISE

> Think of examples where you have implemented plans to work *'smarter'*
>
> - _____
> - _____
> - _____
>
> What were the benefits gained?
>
> - _____
> - _____
> - _____

One principle is to set out what you can and can't do, and to apply this to other sales-related roles! If you are the business owner, a sales director, manager or sales executive, it can be challenging to adopt a relaxed approach at times when you might be under considerable pressure. That is why it is important to look at ways in which you can be productive. This will involve the need to have good communication and effective working relationships with others.

To support this, have internal business processes which are aligned to your sales strategy (see Chapter 4, *Getting the best out of a sales CRM system)*. Technology alone won't do the job for you, but it can often save you valuable time. Pressure is often built up by many people because they don't feel that they have time to carry out all the tasks required of them. Or they force themselves to do tasks in an unrealistic timeframe.

It is also important to be aware of what you like and don't like, and what you can and can't accept in relation to your own role. This has to take into consideration the areas you are directly involved with on a day-to-day basis.

PRACTICAL POINTER

If you are the business owner, you might feel you have to accept some of the workload and pressures of others, whether you like it or not. But this will make your own work/life balance harder to achieve!

Rather than accept every stressful situation, see if tasks can be handled in a different way, or delegated. This in itself has to be managed as there is a difference between delegation and abdication! If you have a sales director or sales manager you might want to look at how well you delegate tasks. The person who has a task delegated to them needs to feel that they can cope with it and that it is relevant to their job role.

If tasks can be delegated appropriately it is a good example of 'working smarter'. There are also cases where if someone is being developed in a particular role, he/she might welcome this, providing it doesn't put that person under too much pressure.

This can help to reduce levels of stress for the business owner and give you the correct balance between work and a home life. There are other ways in which you can manage this; for example, set yourself goals in your home life that are not work related. This also applies to everyone in the sales operation.

Consider what *'success'* actually means to you at work; is it mainly target driven? Think about the company's sales objectives and compare these to your own subjective, personal goals.

A key point is to think about what you *can* do to get the work/life balance right. You will not always be able to work less hard, but you can look at ways to continue to be effective in order to lessen any pressure you might feel. To appreciate this more, it can be helpful to list how you spend your time during a typical working week. To look at this, complete the following table:

EXERCISE: YOUR WORKING WEEK

Type of activity	Amount of time spent	Percentage of time (of the total hours in a week)
Internal meetings	Meetings with customers/target accounts	
Meetings with suppliers		
Planning		
Phone calls		
Travelling		
Entertaining/lunch		
Other (list)		

This type of information will help you to form a more balanced view of how you spend your time and how you might spend it better. It will help you to judge whether you feel in control of your time or if you feel that time is controlling you! If it is the latter, you will need to be more assertive and look at ways in which you can manage yourself (and other employees better).

The people in your sales operation should have an opportunity to discuss their *work/life balance* at a *Progress and Development* review. The challenges will be different if you are the business owner. In this case you might seek advice from an experienced colleague or another director you know and respect. You could also promote a discussion with your own management team as to how you can improve your sales operation's structure and processes in order to increase efficiency and productivity.

Managing stress

For many companies under pressure, the best managerial practices can be tested to the limit, which can lead to stress at every level. Managing this type of situation can help to reduce conflict and maintain stability.

Most people would agree that a continued amount of stress isn't good for your health, your company or your personal relationships. It is also a major contributory factor in upsetting the work/life balance.

James (2006) noted how 'longer hours in an increasingly competitive, complex and technologically speeded-up economy has become overwhelming.' He described many people who put a high value on money and possessions as having an *Affluenza* virus. This, he argued, placed these types of people open to 'a greater risk of depression and anxiety'.

Dissatisfaction at work can also lead to employee absence and poor performance. This will lead to more pressure for everyone, so understanding people in sales roles, can improve the quality of the work they do. This, along with meeting your business objectives, will help to motivate them in order to help fulfill their sales potential.

Some of the home life factors which should be considered include:

- Having a support infrastructure at home (friends/family).
- Having a good diet and regular exercise.
- Having leisure interests in your social time.
- Getting enough sleep.
- Knowing what type of *work/life balance* you actually need.
- Generally trying to feel positive about life!

Pressures at work lead to stress and, in some cases, this can cause employees to leave and business owners to be less effective.

PRACTICAL POINTER

It is more costly to have a high turnover of staff than retain good people by creating a harmonious working environment!

In order to help manage any pressure you might feel complete the following exercise.

EXERCISE

Think of ways that you can relieve pressures at work:

- _____
- _____
- _____

Also think about how you can do this for others:

- _____
- _____
- _____

Think about what sales and customer service training, coaching and management development people might need. This will require some investment of your time and money, but it will encourage people to develop in a way that you want. This should help them to grow in their role, be more loyal and produce the results you are looking for.

You will want to ensure that a sales team, in particular, reach their sales targets without feeling anxious all the time. People in selling roles tend to be outgoing and hungry for success. Managing them well will increase their chances of meeting their targets as well as the business objectives. This will be something that you will want to get right to ensure your company is a relatively happy one to work for.

By getting your *work/life balance* right you will be better prepared to deal with any work-related stress. Another consideration is the different types of business relationships we form at work and the roles and responsibilities of each person.

Roles and responsibilities

The relationship business owners have with employees (and their level of responsibility) is a key part of building a successful sales operation. This section considers these relationships, as well as the dangers of being over-reliant on a particular individual or specialist.

In today's competitive environment, good business relationships at work are essential at all levels, especially in a sales operation. They can be challenging, when people are under pressure as they may not always have empathy for someone else's job role.

There is likely to be closer daily interaction between colleagues in an SME compared to a larger company. This might be because there may only be one office and one single business owner. However, you should try and ensure that you have the right people in the right role! This can be challenging, especially if a perfect fit isn't easily attainable.

PRACTICAL POINTER

In any job role, try and fit the person to the role rather than the role to the person!

If you don't follow this practice you may have people who are in the wrong job role. If this does happen (especially if a person is a specialist or in a key support role), it can influence others in a negative way.

Over-reliance on people

Business owners need to be mindful of the type of role they give someone in a sales operation and of how that person interacts with others. Be particularly careful about the type of people you place in a role with a low level of authority, but a high level of responsibility! This is because they can have a significant amount of control over a sales team without you always realising.

You need to ensure that if you rely on someone in this type of role, he/she doesn't take advantage of that position. If their influence becomes negative, that person has the ability to disrupt the team and lower morale.

This type of over-dependency can cause problems which can seriously affect your sales potential. If the person performing a role like this isn't team-orientated or is overworked, it can undermine good business relationships at work and lead to a breakdown in communication.

Business owners being over reliant on people generally can also become an issue. For example, if successful sales executives leave, they might be tempted to encourage an existing customer to do business with their new company.

Do you manage anyone who you are over-reliant on and who oversteps the boundaries of authority? If so, consider other departments which interact with the sales team to ensure that you are aware of anyone like this, for example:

1. IT/technical.

2. Finance/accounts.
3. Sales administration.
4. Sales support.
5. Service/technical.

It is often the hardest working members of staff who take on too much. This can lead to people not doing a job well, becoming stressed and at times being ineffective! To focus on this, complete the following exercise:

EXERCISE

> **Does this happen in your company?**
> **If so, what do you think the solutions are?**
>
> - _____
> - _____
> - _____
> - _____
> - _____
> - _____

If someone oversteps the boundaries in their role or is working too hard, talk to their manager – and if that is you, put a plan in place to correct this. Be positive – set realistic goals, outcomes and timeframes to achieve the changes you are looking for. Try to understand why this type of situation has arisen. For example, factors that can affect employee relations in a situation like this include:

- The sales systems and processes you have in place.
- The structure of your company and its culture.
- How good and experienced your sales executives are.
- Whether your sales targets are being met.
- The interaction of different personalities in the sales operation.
- The level of self-discipline of an individual (and your own level of tolerance).

Working with people often requires different strategies and approaches. You must set the standards which you expect others to follow in terms of your leadership and management style.

Internal interpersonal relationships need to take into account the nature of someone's character because inequality can lead to division. It is natural to find some dominant personalities in a sales operation. A certain amount of individuality is good and is often part of being successful. It is how any potential conflicts are managed however, which often forms part of the reasons behind a company's success.

The amount of delegation and control a business owner uses is also a key determinant of how well a company is run. This is where the relationship between harmony at work and sales results plays an important role.

Chapter summary

This chapter covered two main areas:

- Work/life balance.
- Roles and responsibilities.

In order to maintain a healthy *work/life balance* you need to decide what balance is good for you and look at how to achieve this. The pressure and responsibilities you face can affect your home life, and a business owner needs to manage this. The level of control you feel you have over your sales operation will go some way to helping you to manage your levels of potential stress.

If you have employees in your sales operation who work hard but are not pulling in the same direction as other people, look to address this. It will improve team morale and help the company to achieve its sales objectives. Getting the right balance in these areas will also help to create a harmonious and productive working environment.

Key points

- ✓ Determine what type of *work/life balance* you want and what is realistic.
- ✓ Manage yourself effectively so that you don't work longer hours than you have to.
- ✓ Being stressed is not healthy, so if you experience this regularly, delegate some of your responsibilities.
- ✓ Don't become too dependent on one person and don't let others become over-dependent on you.

Bibliography

Bibliography

Chapter 1 – Responding to changes in the market

- Strategic Drift, Managing Strategic Change, Strategy, Culture and Action
  – G. Johnson (1992).

- Matrix Position Map
  – D. Mercer (1996).

- Scenario Planning
  – P. Wack and T. Newland (1975).

- The Psychological Contract
  – S.L. Robinson and D.M. Rousseau (1994).

- Shared Values
  – R.M. Kanter (1997).

- The Cultural Webb
  – G. Johnson (1988).

- Precepts
  – J. N. T. Martin (2000).

- The Magical Number 7 Plus or Minus 2
  – G. Miller (1956).

Chapter 2 – Creating a sales and marketing strategy

- Generic Strategies
  – M. Porter (1980).

- Ansoff's Matrix
  – I. Ansoff (1957).

- The Marketing Mix
  – N. Borden (1953).

- The Four P's
  – E. J. McCarthy (1960).

- The Boston Matrix
  – Boston Consulting Group (1968).

- Vision, the Definition
  – E. Métayer (2004).

Chapter 3 – Implementing your strategy (with a sales operations plan)

- Training, Evaluation and Follow up
  – M. Easterby-Smith (1998).

- Double Loop Learning
  – Argyris and Schon (1978).

Chapter 4 – Getting the best out of a sales CRM system

- A Mathematical Theory of Communication
  – C. E. Shannon (1948).

- Assessing Your Company's Knowledge Management Style
  – P. Jordan and P. Jones (1997).

- What You Know You Don't Know
  – Jordan et al (1998).

Chapter 5 – How to improve your decision-making

- Behavioural Studies for Marketing and Business
  – F. Spooncer (1992).

- An Experimental Study of Apparent Behaviour
  – F. Heider and M. Simmel (1944).

- The Behaviour of Organisms
  – B. F. Skinner (1938).

- The Ego and the Mechanisms of Defence
  – A. Freud (1936).

- Social Identity Theory
  – H. Tajfel (1971).

- The Psychology of Personal Constructs
  – G. Kelly (1955).

- Attribution Theory in Social Psychology
  – H. H. Kelley (1967).

- Young Girl, Old Woman Illusion
  – W.E. Hill (1915). (Note: original artist unknown (1888).)

- Visual Figures
  – E. Rubin (1915).

- The Müller-Lyer Illusion
  – F.C. Müller-Lyer (1889).

Chapter 6 – A strategy for managing different types of people

- Stakeholder Power Matrix
  – D. Winstanley, D. Sorabji, S. Dawson (1995).

- The Original Nine Dot Problem, Cyclopedia of Puzzles
  – S. Loyd (1914), Interpreted by M. Scheerer (1963).

- The Scientific Analysis of Personality and Motivation
  – R. B. Cattell and P Kline (1977).
- The Biological Basis of Personality
  – H. J. Eysenck (1967).

Chapter 7 – Teamwork and communication

- Theory of Games and Economic Behaviour
  – J. von Neumann and O. Morgenstern (1944).
- Prisoner's Dilemma
  – R. Powers (1988).
- Social Identity Theory
  – H. Tajfel (1971).
- Reinforcement-Affect Theory
  – D. Byrne and G. L. Core (1970).
- Games People Play: the Psychology of Human Relationships
  – Eric Berne (1964).
- I'm OK, You're OK
  – T. Harris (1967).

Chapter 8 – Working more productively

- Critique of Economic Reason
  – A. Gorz (1989).
- Affluenza
  – O. James (2007).